Praise for
Mission Possible

"Tim is the perfect author for a book that encourages readers to make their lives count. The principles he talks about reflect not only his passion but also the vision for his life that he actively pursues. When you take this journey through these pages with Tim, one thing is clear: You're going to discover purpose wherever you are and leave an impact wherever you go. If you want to do much more than just occupy space in this life, pick up this book and let Tim show you how."

—THOMAS RHETT AKINS, country music artist
and 2021 ACM Awards Male Artist of the Year

"For years I've watched my friend Tim Tebow pursue various passions—each of them with all his heart, mind, and strength. No matter the challenges or opinions he faced, his faith in the greater purpose was unwavering. His perseverance remains the same today, and I believe *Mission Possible* will help you know why you, too, can embody that mindset in whatever passion you're pursuing."

—STEPHEN A. SMITH, sports journalist, radio host,
and ESPN commentator

"No matter who you are or where you are from, God has a plan for your life. Understanding His plan can become quite challenging for those who aren't equipped with the right tools. *Mission Possible* will help you deal with what God has in store for you. Tim allows us to see that God's plan has purpose even though we may not see it clearly at times."

—LUKE BRYAN, country music artist
and five-time ACM Awards Entertainer of the Year

"*Mission Possible* is timely and timeless. Each chapter is written with intentionality, emphasizing a sense of urgency to discover what it means to make your life count. It doesn't matter your background, title, zip code, or perceived limitations; Tim reminds you that God created us all to live each day with purpose. And in this book, Tim will show you how. When you turn the final page, get ready to be, as he calls it, 'a champion of higher purpose.'"

—STEVEN FURTICK, *New York Times* bestselling author
and pastor of Elevation Church

Mission Possible
Young Reader's Edition

Mission Possible
Young Reader's Edition

+ + +

Go Create a Life That Counts

Tim Tebow

with A. J. Gregory

WaterBrook

Contents

Introduction

I'm often asked, "What is God's will for my life?" Or sometimes it's phrased like this: "How can I find my calling?" or "What is my purpose?"

I've often wondered what we even mean when we use those words. I know how they are defined in the dictionary, but what do they really mean to us? Is it about choosing a specific career or making a difference? Does it have anything to do with faith? (Am I asking too many new questions when you're hoping to find answers?)

This whole thing reminds me of a funny conversation in *The Hobbit*. After finishing breakfast, Bilbo Baggins is standing by his front door, when none other than Gandalf comes waltzing by. Bilbo nods at the old wizard and says, "Good morning!" It's a typical early-day greeting that requires nothing more than a nod and a smile. But Gandalf is too deep for that.

He says to Bilbo, "Do you wish me a good morning, or mean that it is a good morning whether I want it or not; or that you feel good this morning; or that it is a morning to be good on?"[1]

I suppose we each have a little bit of Gandalf in us. We can get hung up on questions instead of taking action.

The Bible gives us one shared and big-picture purpose: to glorify God. As believers, we honor and serve Him with our lives, our natural gifts, the choices we make, and our time. The goal is clear. In His last instructions to His disciples, Jesus commanded them to "go, therefore, and make disciples of all the nations, baptizing them in the name of the Father and the Son and the Holy Spirit, teaching them to follow all that I commanded you; and behold, I am with you always, to the end of the age" (Matthew 28:19–20).

Jesus wasn't telling us to become career missionaries or plant ourselves on the other side of the world. Nor was He saying that we have to sing worship songs every second of every day. But these verses do mean that your big-picture purpose is to bring glory to God wherever you are. Right now. Not when you get your driver's license or graduate from high school. Today!

Within that greater purpose of glorifying God, we find our purpose in what we do every day. Living a mission-possible life means doing the good works that God has already prepared for us to do.

This is what Paul was talking about when he wrote, "We are His workmanship, created in Christ Jesus for good works, which God prepared beforehand so that we would walk in them" (Ephesians 2:10). We can live mission-possible lives today because of what Jesus did for us on the cross more than two thousand years ago. This kind of life is possible only because of the sacrifice He made and the power given to Him to trample over death. When you live mission possible, you live a life that counts because of what God has done and is doing through you.

We are each on a mission to make a difference: a mission to

help the hurting; a mission to reach the last, the lost, and the least. It looks different for everyone, and it's a lot easier than you think. Have you ever been going about your day, when suddenly, out of nowhere, you start thinking of someone and wonder how they are? Or you watch a commercial and your heart is touched by a need? Does your heart ache for the kid in your class who always gets picked on? The world is flooded with hurting people and messed-up situations. And while we cannot fix every problem, God can. What we can do, with His help, is bring some light to a world that is shadowed with darkness.

I wasn't always driven to help people with special needs. I first felt a pull in that direction when I met a little boy in the Philippines with his feet on backward. From there, my passion grew to help people. That's why in 2010, I was so excited to create the Tim Tebow Foundation (TTF), with a mission to bring faith, hope, and love to those needing a brighter day in their darkest hour of need.[2]

God has a special plan and purpose for you. Yes, you. By using what He has already given you, right where you are, you can make a positive difference in the world. This is my mission, and it's yours too. When you start to live mission possible, you will begin to

- see what's possible with God
- make better decisions that make your life, and other people, count
- live with passion
- understand you have a purpose that reaches beyond today

The greatest lie you may ever hear is that your life doesn't matter. *You're too young. You're not good at anything. Remember what you did last week?* How often do you hear those things whispered in your ear at night when you turn off your phone and lie alone in your bed?

It's hard to live mission possible when we don't fully believe that we are made in God's image, hand-chosen by Him and able to carry out works of eternal significance. It's actually impossible. You will never come to believe that your life counts if you think you are here by accident or if you're stuck in a space where you're just going through the motions.

Lean in a bit. If you have made the decision to trust in Jesus, you're not just an average person who got slightly better. You were someone who was dead in sin who is now alive in Christ. Take a moment and read that again. You were *dead,* and now you are *alive.* Wow!

Through His death and resurrection, Jesus has brought each of us from:

old to new,
dead to alive,
sin to righteousness,
slave to son or daughter,
bondage to freedom,
darkness to light,
lost to found.

I hope that fires you up as much as it does me!

When you believe that you are valuable and worthy because of who lives inside you, everything changes. You find meaning. You live with purpose. And when you soak in the truth that you were created in the image of God—by love, in love, and for love—you begin to see the world differently. You see people in a new light. Your eyes open to hurt, and your heart hopes for the hurting.

Tom Cruise gets major props for doing most of his stunts in the *Mission: Impossible* films. He plays Ethan Hunt, an agent of the Impossible Missions Force who, with his spy team, will do whatever it takes to save the world. As Ethan Hunt, Cruise engages in stunts that require serious training, defy gravity, and risk death.

In *Ghost Protocol*, Cruise scales and hangs off the tallest building in the world: a Dubai skyscraper that stands 2,716 feet tall. Oh, and he's using only a pair of climbing gloves to do it. We find Cruise fiddling with an underwater security system in *Rogue Nation* and having to hold his breath for six minutes. (The average person can hold his or her breath for one or two minutes.) The same movie features Cruise dangling off an Airbus A400M while it takes off, reaches an altitude of about five thousand feet at 184 miles per hour, and then lands.[3] (He was wearing a harness, but still.) Then there's the opening scene in *Mission: Impossible 2*—the one where Cruise hangs from a cliff with his bare hands. He was fitted with a safety harness but refused a safety net.

My favorite scene is found in the first *Mission: Impossible*. It's arguably the most memorable in the franchise. Cruise executes a high-wire dive in the CIA building to hack a computer in a pressure-sensitive and secured vault. Most of the stunt is performed by Cruise. It's his core and balance at work while being suspended in one position, perfectly still.

These stunts seem impossible for most of us. I don't know many people who could hang off the edge of a cliff by their hands or who would even want to try.

The good news is that when God is involved, it's always mission possible. Jesus may not have been pushed out of a plane at twenty-five thousand feet, but He did something even more daring: He defeated death. And if you are serving a God who has rattled the doors of hell and trampled over death, you can fulfill whatever He has called you to do.

In this book, I'm going to show you how to make your life count for God and for others and how to live each day with a greater purpose. I want to remind you that you are a masterpiece. That's right! You are God's masterpiece. You were created to do good things, in your own unique way, on your own unique journey.

Our time on earth is so short. I want to do things that matter. I'm so honored to be able to play sports, write books, and motivate others. But I'm most passionate about bringing faith, hope, and love to those needing light in their darkest hour through the work we do at my foundation. I try to live out of that passion, trusting that when I fall short or don't have a map for what's next, God has it all under control.

We serve a God who is much bigger than an impressive character in a fictional movie. We serve the God of this universe, who holds life itself in His hands. He is in this with you. He is beside you. He is rooting for you, and He is fighting for you. Remember, with Him, all things are possible. What are you waiting for?

Let's take that first step, together!

Mission Possible
Young Reader's Edition

1

Mission Proposal, Mission Purpose

I've always believed the mission is greater than the man.
—RICK PERRY

The Sierra Madre has one of the largest rain forests in the Philippines. Situated on the island of Luzon, this rugged jungle is home to a surviving hunter-gatherer group called the Agta. Several years ago, a team of anthropologists set out to study this Indigenous group of people. The researchers were curious to learn more about how the Agta valued the members of their tribe based on their individual contributions. They discovered that out of all the different trades and talents these people possessed, including fishing and cooking, the people the Agta held in highest regard were storytellers.[1] Imagine that! The folks who spun tales had a higher status than those who literally brought home the bacon (and the snacks and drinks).

But most of us love a good story, don't we? Stories matter. They keep us entertained. They can carry on family traditions through generations. Stories can engage and inspire a single life or go on to change thousands.

When I began to think about how to propose to my then girlfriend, Demi, I knew it had to be a great story. I wanted to offer my future bride an experience that she would never forget, one that would make butterflies flutter in her stomach each time she retold it. Okay, fine, and maybe, just maybe, there was smidgen of ego in my motivation. I wanted to be the awesome fiancé who crushed this monumental task. (What can I say? I'm a competitive guy, even with myself.)

There were three things this story had to have: special people, a beautiful location, and the element of surprise. The goal was to have a mission-possible mission proposal for the girl of my dreams.

The ring had to come from Africa, my bride's homeland. I met with a jeweler who recommended an "internally flawless diamond," which is exactly what it sounds like. It was also responsibly sourced and had a story of its own—how and where it was discovered and the detailed processes it underwent to be crafted—recorded in a beautifully designed book.

Giving gifts is my love language. Having found a woman who to me was the epitome of flawless beauty in so many ways, I knew this was the ring for her.

I had found something beautiful to give to the love of my life. Now to create the element of surprise. Unbeknownst to my bride,

I had arranged for my family, both sets of Demi's parents, and her best friends to be present the moment I popped the question. Special people? Check.

The big moment would come on January 9, after a belated and (wink, wink!) pretend Christmas celebration with my family in Florida. Over the actual holidays, I was helping to cover the national championship between Clemson and Alabama for *SEC Nation* and ESPN. Demi and I flew from South Africa, where we had spent Christmas, to the States. At the ESPN party before the big game on January 7, Demi and I met the president of Clemson, Jim Clements, and his wife, Beth. They are some of the sweetest people you'll ever meet. They have four children, including a daughter named Grace, who has special needs, and host a Night to Shine event in their community. (I'll talk more about Night to Shine in a later chapter.) The four of us became fast friends. Fast-forward to the pregame show. Right after filming for *SEC Nation*, I looked around and noticed Demi was nowhere to be found. I sent her a text saying I had to be down on the field for the first part of the game but that we could meet up after. Her reply was shocking: "That's fine! I'm hanging out with Jim and Beth in their box!"

What? As a good southern boy would say, "Bless her heart." I mean, Jim and Beth are absolutely wonderful people, but Demi doesn't understand American football allegiances! While I don't necessarily root for Alabama, I do work for *SEC Nation*. But Demi's decision to hang with the Clementses says a lot about her. Even if she had understood the difference between the Atlantic Coast Conference (ACC) and the Southeastern Conference (SEC), it wouldn't have mattered to her. She appreciates people just for who they are. It's one of many reasons I fell in love with her.

Demi and I arrived in Jacksonville, Florida, my hometown, on January 8. We spent the next day celebrating "kid Christmas" first. All the nieces and nephews gathered at my house and unwrapped their gifts, and then it was time for the adults to unwrap their gifts, one person at a time, one gift at a time. After each gift, we took time to talk about it. You can imagine how long the process took.

In order to create a proposal that was unexpected, I did something that you might think is borderline unfair. As we opened presents with my family that morning, I gave Demi a small velvet box. I knew what she really was hoping to find in that box, even though she'd never say it out loud. When the box clicked open, Demi's eyes widened and she beheld . . . not an engagement ring. I figured getting her a non-engagement ring would take care of any expectations she had of getting a real one. To her credit, Demi was so gracious about her gift.

We continued unwrapping presents for a while. Once we finished, it was time for Mission Proposal, which would happen in the backyard of my parents' farmhouse. The plan was for everyone to meet for dinner at my parents' house nearby. Some of the women suggested to Demi that she dress up since Christmas dinner at the Tebows' was a formal thing (not true, by the way—more like jeans and T-shirts or pajamas). I had something else planned to further throw Demi off the scent of an engagement. A friend who worked at a local car dealership had dropped off a decoy truck that Demi and I were going to drive over to my parents' to give my father as his last gift. After the engagement actually happened, I'd return the truck to the dealership. (Sorry, Dad!) The day was full with sweet surprises but none (yet) for my soon-to-be fiancée. I was positive Demi had zero clue of getting engaged that day.

Funny, on the drive over to my parents' place, one of our favorite songs just happened to come on. It was "The Wedding Song" by Demi's favorite South African artist, Matthew Mole—the very same musician I had flown in that day and had arranged to play live for her right after I asked her to marry me. The mood was perfectly set.

The engagement and post-engagement pictures had to be taken during the last hour before sunset so the lighting could hit just right with the backyard scenery. Photographers had camouflaged themselves behind trees and bushes. Microphones had been planted in secret so our loved ones back at the house could be a part of the moment and be ready to join us on cue.

Finally, it was time. We pulled into the farm but didn't go inside the packed house. Instead, I asked Demi to follow me behind the house, where the pond was. I told her I had something to show her. The sun hung low on the horizon. Crickets chirped in the background, and a slight breeze whispered on our skin. Beautiful location? Check.

So many fond memories flooded my mind as the pond came into view. Demi knew the pond was special to me. It was where our family buried Otis, the dog I grew up with. And it would be where, ten months later, I would bury Bronco, my next dog. By that pond, I had prayed about where to go to college. And now another event was emerging that would change the course of both of our lives. Demi and I walked to a wooden archway adorned with white flowers. Underneath was a bench, and under the bench I had carved the following to mark the span of our dating relationship:

Timmy & Demi
4/28/2018–1/9/2019
Forever . . . My Sweets

I spoke from the heart. I can't tell you everything that was said, because that's just between me and her, but here are the lines that mean the most and I'll remember always: "Demi, I love you so much. I wanted to come here, to where I grew up, to a place that I love so much, with the person I love the most. When I first saw you, you gave me so much hope. When I first heard your voice, you gave me so much belief. When I first met you, I knew I wanted to spend the rest of my life fighting for you, fighting for us." I slipped down to the ground on one knee. "Will you marry me?"

She said yes.

After shedding a few tears and sharing some laughs, we held each other close as "The Wedding Song" played. It was a cue for the next scene in the story. As tears drenched Demi's eyes, a figure began to emerge from a stack of hay bales. It was Matthew Mole himself, strumming his guitar and serenading us live. Demi's face froze in shock. There he was, her favorite artist, playing for her right there in Jacksonville.

Matthew was also the second cue. As Demi and I swayed in rhythm to the melody, I gently turned us around so the back deck of the house was out of her view. "I wish your family could be here right now," I whispered.

Demi nodded. "Me too," she said, sadness in her eyes. We danced while the sun continued its descent under the horizon. After a minute or two, I turned her around and she burst into tears. Her parents and their spouses were walking toward us with arms outstretched. Third cue. During the tearful reunion, three of Demi's closest friends came out of the house and joined the tear fest. Fourth cue. Finally, my parents and sisters and brothers made their way toward the wooden archway. As our loved ones followed their cues, photographers leaped from behind their hiding places and snapped forever memories of the happy occasion. Demi was visibly overwhelmed. She looked radiant, perfectly happy. Just seeing her shine in that moment was worth every minute of planning and secrecy. The proposal unfolded exactly on schedule and exactly as planned.

I'll never forget what Demi told my dad when the night came to a close. "Mr. Tebow, I'm sorry you didn't get your truck, but you're getting a new daughter!"

Mission accomplished.

When I look back on the effort, thought, and time I invested in creating a story Demi would be excited to retell a thousand times in the future, I clearly remember the sense of urgency I had. While the grand gesture—the proposal itself—mattered, of course, the little gestures along the way were just as important. In the months before I asked Demi to marry me, I spent time each day doing a task, however small, to accomplish my mission.

Now, while I don't approach every day with this much intention and focus and detail, there's something to be learned about how mission driven I was in proposing to Demi. Focusing our attention on the right things serves us well. I want this to be the way I live my entire life, including how I love Demi, serve and inspire others, pursue my dreams, and honor God. I don't want to be just a football player or an author or commentator, even though I love doing all those things and work hard at them. But I want my life to be so much more than that. I want to live a mission-possible life. I want to always strive to bring faith, hope, and love to those needing a brighter day in their darkest hour. That's the mission statement of our foundation, and it's also my personal mission statement.

When you strive to make your life count, you think less about how others see you and more about what God thinks. You realize that how you actually live has a greater impact than just putting your best self on social media so you can rack up the likes.

We are meant to do so much more than take up space or look good. We are called to love, care, pitch in, carry the burdens of others, and fight for those who can't fight for themselves.

A mission-possible life has less to do with us and more to do with others. Mission living means being motivated by something other than yourself. It's scary. But it's also pretty exciting. It can be unpredictable (but in a good way). It will require submitting your preferences to God. That means you choose His best over what you'd prefer, which isn't always easy. This is where trusting God becomes crucial. If you've made the decision to trust Him, He gives you the mission and makes it possible. Trust that He's got better plans for your life than you do.

Purpose over Preference

A man named Jonah learned that the hard way. In the Old Testament, Jonah was a prophet from the nation of Israel. Today I'd call him a foreign missionary. One day, God gave this prophet a mission:

> Arise, go to Nineveh, the great city, and cry out against it, because their wickedness has come up before Me. (Jonah 1:2)

The people who lived in the city of Nineveh, the capital of the ancient empire of Assyria, needed a come-to-Jesus awakening. This nation had long been a threat to Israel, and they weren't living right. God had given Jonah a simple task: to preach. But apparently this didn't align with the prophet's preferences. Jonah hated the Ninevites. They were cruel, mean bullies, and in Jonah's eyes, they deserved to be destroyed, not given a chance to repent. God said, "Preach!" but Jonah ran instead.

So Jonah ran to a local port, bought a ticket, and set sail with other passengers for the city of Tarshish—in the opposite direction from Nineveh. Then God sent a powerful storm to get the prophet's attention. The raging wind and pounding rain whipped the ship without mercy, threatening to break it apart. The sailors on board threw their cargo into the sea to lighten the load and prayed to their false gods for help. And Jonah? Well, he was curled up in his bed, fast asleep and clutching his blankie.

The sailors wanted help from whatever god might possibly be listening. They woke Jonah up and begged him to pray to whomever he worshipped. Then they interrogated him. *Who are you? Where are you from? What are you doing here? Whom do you serve?* Realizing the storm wasn't leaving anytime soon, Jonah fessed up and admitted the storm was probably his fault. Then he suggested they toss him overboard. Some of them probably thought that wasn't the worst idea they'd ever heard, but they still hesitated at first. Eventually, they got desperate and pitched Jonah into the sea. And wouldn't you know it, the instant his shivering body hit the water, there were clear blue skies.

I don't know how good a swimmer the prophet was, but he must have been freaking out while treading in waters so deep he couldn't see the bottom. Then, as Jonah gasped for breath, a great fish shimmied up and swallowed him whole, and he stayed in the creature's belly for three whole days. Before Jonah checked out of his aquatic Airbnb, he cried out to God and repented. Then God nudged the fish again and it vomited Jonah out onto the shore. (I know, gross.)

Before Jonah had time to take a very long shower, God repeated his mission: "Arise, go to Nineveh, the great city, and proclaim to it the proclamation which I am going to tell you" (3:2). This time Jonah wised up and preached to the entire city. It was one of the most successful revivals in the Bible. Even the king repented. And instead of destroying the city because of its evil ways,

God poured out compassion, love, and forgiveness. You'd think Jonah would be thrilled. But he wasn't. He basically told God that he wished he were dead.

Here's what was going on in Jonah's mind: He was a prophet, so his job was to say things that were supposed to come true. Jonah had preached destruction to the city of Nineveh before, but God, who is filled with kindness and mercy, changed His mind. He didn't want to destroy the Ninevites; He wanted to show them His love. For Jonah, however, as a prophet, doing so was going to make him look bad. The prophet was more concerned about what his fellow Israelites would think of him than about God fulfilling His greatest mission on earth: saving humankind.

I think deep down many of us can relate to Jonah. Have you ever been afraid to make a difference for God because it might make you stick out or look weird? Have you ever not done something He wanted you to do because you knew others would probably tell you it was dumb? You may not win a popularity contest by being mission driven, but you'll certainly gain the favor of your Father in heaven. And isn't that what counts?

I admire my dad's boldness now, but that wasn't always the case. I remember that the few times we went out to eat as a family growing up, we'd always pray before the meal. For most people, this means huddling up, bowing your heads, and whispering a short and simple pre-dinner prayer. But Dad would blast his prayers so loud that the patrons three tables over would hear, "Because you alone, O Lord, walk on the wings of the wind" (see Psalm 104:3). I hate to say this, but there were times I'd slink low in my seat and cringe. Dad was never ashamed of making his faith known, because Jesus was always the most important thing to him. He didn't care if it made him look strange. Eventually I grew to admire and respect that about him and would get irritated at the people who made fun of him for it (and there were many).

If we want to make our lives count, we have to be a little different. We have to do things a little differently. Why would we want to be like everyone else?

Living a life of significance is more valuable than other people thinking well of you. Whenever you are forced to make a decision between purpose and preference, choose purpose. It'll win every time.

Live Like You're Running Out of Time

A few years ago, I was covering the Heisman ceremony for ESPN in New York City, where Demi, my fiancée at the time, lived. As crammed as our schedules were, I knew it'd be a real miss if I didn't plan something fun for us to do. At the last minute, I got tickets to see the Broadway show *Hamilton*.

Lin-Manuel Miranda wrote this unique retelling of the story of Alexander Hamilton, one of America's founding fathers. Hamilton helped write the Constitution and was the first secretary of the United States Treasury and the creator of the American financial system. As Lin-Manuel put it, "This is a story about America then, told by America now."[2]

To say I loved *Hamilton* is an understatement. The songs, the ideas, the acting—can it get any better? This actually was my third time seeing the show. But I was going to walk out of that theater after the final curtain fell feeling God prick my heart. And it would respark a mission.

Alexander Hamilton was a beast when it came to writing. Act 1 of *Hamilton* closes with a song called "Non-stop." After the Revolutionary War, Hamilton partnered up with John Jay and James Madison and between October 1787 and May 1788 wrote what came to be called the Federalist Papers. The eighty-five essays were published anonymously and for the purpose of defending the Constitution. John Jay wrote five, James Madison wrote twenty-nine, and Alexander Hamilton wrote fifty-one. The song "Non-stop" captures Hamilton's stubbornness and persistence. When the character Hamilton started singing the part about writing "like you're running out of time," I knew that God wanted me to hear something special.

> *How do you write like you're running out of time?*
> *Write day and night like you're running out of time?*
> *Every day you fight, like you're running out of time*
> *Like you're running out of time.*[3]

Those lyrics played in my head for the rest of the show but in a different way. I heard,

> *How do you live like you're running out of time?*
> *Do you fight for people like you're running out of time?*
> *How do you love Jesus like you're running out of time?*
> *Do you live like you need Him to survive?*

I am inspired by Hamilton's passion and fire for pioneering revolutionary legislation and defending the cause of independence. This was a good and important cause, one that was historically necessary. But it's not a greater cause than the cause of Christ. Hamilton was fighting to defend the Constitution of the United States. We, as believers of the Truth, are fighting to shine light in darkness.

After the musical, my attention turned inward. I truly felt in the bottom of my heart a sense of urgency about how I was living my life, more than I ever had before. Centuries from now, are people going to be talking about my life, my choices, and my work with the same kind of passion and urgency? Would they say that I cared about people? Would they point to the fact that I lived on purpose? It's not so much that I care about what others think or say about me but that I want my life and legacy to speak volumes about how much Jesus loves this world.

If we truly believe in whose we are and know that people are hurting in a dark place, we must feel a sense of urgency to get to them and share with them faith, hope, and love. Does your life actually show a sense of urgency in what you believe?

If not, what might look different if it did?

Look Outside Yourself

Twenty-three-year-old Jaden Barr has had type 1 diabetes since he was fifteen years old, as well as reoccurring cholesteatoma, which has resulted in hearing loss in both ears. While he admits he has made mistakes and fallen short time and time again, Jaden desires to live a life that glorifies God and make the most of the time he's been given.

I met Jaden in 2015 through our foundation's W15H (pronounced "wish") program. I spent a few days with this amazing young man. We even had the chance to work out together. Part of my mission was to encourage him, but by the end of our time together, he was the one encouraging me! Funny how God works that way so often.

In light of the health challenges Jaden has had to endure, he recognizes what it means to live a mission-possible life:

> Without a clear mission, you're aimlessly going through life without intent or purpose. Experiencing firsthand the mission of the Tim Tebow Foundation has continually reminded me that God created me with a purpose: to know Him and to make Him known. It's easy to fall into the temptation of thinking life is about me and my plans, but I'm always reminded that the mission I've been given by God is much bigger and better than any worldly pursuit. By giving God control over my plans and following His instead, it makes the work I do have meaning and significance.

Right on, Jaden. This incredible young man truly has a heart that desires the greater things, what Jesus called "the good part" (Luke 10:42), or as the New Living Translation puts it, the "one thing worth being concerned about." And what exactly is that one thing? Pursuing God, sitting at His table, being in His presence without worry, fear, anxiety, popularity building, or winning a title. It's not that we never think about those things, but we don't let them dominate our vision. We strive and strain forward in this life with Jesus as our focus, with His will as our goal, and with His rewards as our prize.

My friend Jaden knows the dangers of living for himself. Life can't be all about us. This is tempting for all of us, no matter if we're young or old, a parent or a preacher, a student or a teacher. I love what Jaden once shared with me:

> You'll end up empty if you make life or your mission about yourself. I feel most fulfilled and in line with my purpose when I'm looking outside of myself and my own desires and putting that energy into pouring into others. When you look outside yourself, that's where true mission is found.

Both Jaden and my engagement to Demi remind me of the power and passion that comes when you focus your energy outside of yourself. I want to live each day more alive and more passionate because of what Jesus has done for me. The past—His death and resurrection—keeps me motivated in the present to change the future.

When you get tired or overwhelmed or uncertain, don't forget when God changed your life. If you're reading this book right now and you don't know Him, that time can be now. Choose to trust Him in this very instant.

Don't forget the moment He challenged you to join the fight. And remember, you have a specific role to play in bringing faith, hope, and love to a world in need.

2

God Possible, Purpose Possible

Looking at them, Jesus said, "With people it is impossible,
but not with God; for all things are possible with God."

—Mark 10:27

A few years ago in Ghana, Africa, a girl was born with spina
bifida (which is a spinal birth defect) and bilateral clubfoot.
People with special needs in Ghana, as in many countries, are
looked down upon and denied basic human rights. Often thought
to be cursed or contagious, these children are used perversely
in religious ceremonies, abandoned by their own parents, or
even killed. But not this baby. She was loved and cared for by her
mother.

Sadly, when this girl was four, her mother died. Naked and
alone, she was ignored by the people who lived in her community. To be clear, they knew she was there, alone and afraid. But
they were so disgusted by her disability that they refused to even
look at her. They treated this orphaned child like a wild dog roam-

ing the streets. As each day passed without her being cared for, the little girl grew weak and malnourished. Nearly a month later, she was found naked and deathly ill by a member of the social welfare office, who arranged for her to be placed in a foster home. The people there knew that her life meant more than what others may have thought.

That same year in Michigan, Shannon and Cameron VanKoevering felt a call on their hearts. They began to pray about adopting one or two boys. But something unsettled their prayers. They felt that God was telling them to wait. Later, they learned of a little girl in Ghana who needed surgery for spina bifida and bilateral clubfoot. The medical care this girl needed was complex and costly. It didn't make sense for the VanKoeverings to move forward with that adoption. They didn't have the money. They were hoping to adopt male siblings. How would it be possible?

Shannon and Cameron will always remember the day they first heard this little girl's name: Christabel, which means "beautiful Christian." In those melodic three syllables, this couple noticed a greater truth: Christ is able.

Not knowing how they would pay for the multiple surgeries and aftercare she required, the couple was understandably overwhelmed. Yet, remembering that Christ is able, they began contributing to her medical expenses. Little did they know the impact this precious little girl would have on their lives. Shannon says, "We fell in love with her beautiful smile, and while we felt 100 percent unqualified to parent a child with this type of disability, we jumped into the great unknown and let God take care of the details."

Two and a half years later, Christabel finally came home to her forever family. She has endured multiple surgeries to correct her feet. However, barring a miracle, she will never be able to walk without assistance. This beautiful girl also continues to struggle with vision problems and cognitive impairment. But the Van-Koeverings trust God in His plan and with the details. They remain encouraged by the truth they heard in their daughter's name: "Christ is able."

More Than You Can Handle

The idea of living a mission-possible life can turn your stomach into knots for many reasons. While most of us want to tune into God's purposes and the needs of others, those needs can overwhelm us. What obstacles lie in front of you that prevent you from taking a step forward and making a difference?

The VanKoeverings knew they wanted to adopt, but when they were given the opportunity to provide a forever home to Christabel, they hesitated, but not because they were selfish people or didn't want to welcome Christabel into their family. They hovered over the idea because the girl had legitimate challenges they were unsure they could push through. Yet Christ is able.

The movie *Elf* tells us that smiling is main character Buddy's favorite thing. I like to think that one of God's favorite things is intervening in the impossible.

God has a habit of making His presence known or intervening in impossible missions. If it can't be done in the natural, if it can't be figured out, if it's a problem without a solution, that's where God often does His best work.

The Bible says that we cannot save ourselves—not by the number of followers we have on social media, not by our good works, not by our high GPAs. We receive the free gift of salvation through what Jesus has done for us on the cross. This is one of the reasons the Son of God said, "The things that are impossible with people are possible with God" (Luke 18:27).

The VanKoeverings didn't know if they could handle everything that would come along with adopting a child with special needs. But God did. He had everything they needed. And in their hearts, they chose to trust and believe that He "is able to do far more abundantly beyond all that we ask or think, according to the power that works within us" (Ephesians 3:20).

When we make the decision to trust God with our lives, we are automatically seated at the table of the humanly impossible. It's not about what we can do; it's about what God can do through us.

Get Overwhelmed by God's Spirit

Are you feeling overwhelmed right now? Maybe you don't know how to start living mission possible. I want you to take a deep breath with me right now. If you feel you're not good enough or too young or that you don't have any special skills or talents, breathe those worries out. God has everything you'll need to do what He has put on your heart. You are in the right place at the right time.

I want you to imagine being overwhelmed by the Spirit of God. When Jesus rose from the dead and was taken to heaven, He promised His disciples that although He would not be with them in body any longer, He would send the Holy Spirit to strengthen and comfort them. The only way to experience the active power of God in our lives is to be filled with the Holy Spirit.

The Holy Spirit is not some weird thing; He is the Spirit of God. All Christ followers have God's Spirit living in them, but not all Christians live filled with the Spirit's power. As believers, the Spirit never leaves us, but when we are disobedient, our sinful behavior can limit the active work of God in our lives. On the other hand, when we obey God's will, we can expect to see the Spirit's fruit in our lives. This is a work in progress. If you are a believer, the Spirit is with you. He is your constant companion. It's pretty crazy, isn't it? The Spirit of God living inside you, filling you with power? That's what makes God's plan for your life possible!

Job 33:4 tells us, "The Spirit of God has made me, and the breath of the Almighty gives me life." Take a minute right now to meditate on that truth. What does it mean to you? What kind of hope does it put in your heart? Does it bring some relief?

Settle yourself into that verse:

The Spirit of God has made me,
And the breath of the Almighty gives me life.

Trade the anxiety, the dread, or the pressure that weighs heavily on your heart for the refreshing truth that God breathes life into you. He doesn't feed you with fear. He doesn't drown you in guilt. He won't force you to do something you can't do without Him. If He is prompting you to do something, He will equip, empower, and encourage you and see that mission to completion.

Here's another truth that can alleviate some of the pressure you feel: I've had many conversations with people who feel the mission they are called to is well beyond their abilities. It's just too big. One person can't end homelessness. One person can't ensure that every child has enough to eat. One person can't make clean water a global reality. Of course not. But mission-possible living doesn't depend on our completing these huge goals. You just do what you can, with what you've got, for the glory of God. For example, my dad's mission is to preach the gospel to every person in the Philippines, but he can't change a single heart. That's God's job. That's the role of the Holy Spirit. My dad is committed to doing his part and leaves the rest to God.

Take a Step and Let God Do the Rest

Human trafficking is a big problem all over the world. It means that people are taken and forced to do things against their will. Though we at the foundation had been serving in anti-human-trafficking efforts for seven years, in 2020 I thought about going public with it. I couldn't shake the feeling that God was calling me in that direction. I didn't think my work would completely end human trafficking. Obviously, I can't do that in my own strength and power. But I could do my part and then watch God turn what seemed impossible into the possible.

I'd like to share the story of one woman who encouraged me

with the truth that no matter how dark a situation, light can somehow find a way to shine forth.

Natalie, whose name has been changed to protect her privacy, was forced to do terrible things by her parents when she was really little. By the time she got to high school, although she was smart and capable and even earned a college scholarship, she was depressed and anxious and suffered from emotional problems as a result of her childhood trauma. Two years into college, the pressure proved too much for her.

A year or two later, Natalie's car broke down on the side of the road. Two older men came by and appeared to take pity on her. They seemed nice and promised they could help her. They offered her a place to stay the night and told her she could even bring her dog with her. It all sounded too good to be true. The two men took her to a modest home in a middle-class neighborhood and moved her into her very own room.

Then they drilled the door shut. These men locked Natalie in the house for months. One day she was able to escape but collapsed in the driveway. Thankfully, a neighbor saw her and called 911. Natalie was admitted to a hospital, where she recovered and was identified by a social worker as a trafficking victim. Natalie was able to find hope and healing with our amazing team of loving counselors and the team at Her Song, a faith-based organization that engages women in healing body, mind, and spirit in a safe community and place to belong.

Today, Natalie, now thirty years old, supports herself and her dog. She is free. She has finished her associate degree and works at the same hospital that identified her as a trafficking victim—

actually, no, a trafficking survivor—using her nursing skills to help others while she continues her education.

I want to fight for girls and boys like Natalie. I want to help stop people from ending up in that terrible situation. The road is long and hard, but I'm committed to staying in the fight and allowing God to do what He wants.

Our mission is not to end all evil. If it were, we would have every right to feel overwhelmed. We don't have the power to end every pain and hurt in this world. But our mission is to honor God as we make a difference wherever and however we can. It's not about what we can do; it's about trusting God for what He can do through us. Living a mission-possible life is not about growing our self-confidence; it's about expanding our God-confidence.

Express Confidence

Over the years, I've learned it's easy to trust God when you're winning championships, when everyone loves you, and when you're scoring touchdowns or swinging home runs. But when your reality is less than your ideal, it is harder to believe that God has it all under control. Disappointments chip away at your confidence.

But we can find joy and purpose in even the darkest places. That's not only something the apostle Paul wrote; it's something he lived. He wrote the book of Philippians to a group of people he loved—people he considered family. Philippians is a pretty cheery book. Paul didn't have to get on them for fighting over who should eat what and when and how as he did in the book of Romans. Instead, this letter overflows with peppy encouragement.

> I am confident of this very thing, that He who began a good work among you will complete it by the day of Christ Jesus. (Philippians 1:6)

> To me, to live is Christ, and to die is gain. (1:21)

And we can't forget one of the most well-known scriptures of all: "I can do all things through Him who strengthens me" (4:13).

Don't you get pumped up just reading those words? I bet if Paul were around today, he'd get flooded with invites to speak at conferences all over the world. The irony is that he was writing these encouraging words from prison. Some scholars say that he was actually cooped up in the basement of a prison where the sewage system was. It was dark, it was dirty, and it stank. And as the odor of human waste and rotten food saturated the air, Paul wrote words that strengthened the spirit of the church in Philippi.

I love how he launched the fourth chapter: "Rejoice in the Lord always; again I will say, rejoice!" (4:4). The word *rejoice* isn't one I use often. I doubt you do, either. When's the last time you said to a friend, "What a beautiful day! Let's rejoice together!"? Never, right? While spending time in my NIV study Bible, I came across an interesting footnote. It substituted "expressing confidence in" for "rejoice in."[1] Expressing confidence made a lot of sense to me.

While imprisoned and facing the possibility of being killed for his faith at any moment, Paul could have written about how anxious, worried, and afraid he was. Instead, he chose to record an expression of his unshakable confidence in God. He wanted other believers to share in that same kind of confidence.

In a time of fear and panic, I want to be someone who expresses confidence in God. I also want this to be true when life is hard and hurts. I need to be confident in God when I'm launching a mission that I'm certain I can't fulfill with my own power. I want to express confidence in God when life feels uncertain. I want to express confidence in God when I'm tired. I want to express confidence in God's plan for me when I feel overwhelmed with the details and lose sight of the vision.

I love how The Message paraphrases it: "Celebrate God all day, every day. I mean, revel in him! Make it as clear as you can to all you meet that you're on their side, working with them and not against them. Help them see that the Master is about to arrive. He could show up any minute!" (4:4–5).

"Celebrate God"—I love that! I'm not promising that your mission-possible journey is going to be easy, but I can say it will be worth it.

Don't stop trusting God when things are dark, dank, and smelly. Don't give up the mission because you don't fully understand it and can't figure out the game plan. When your doubt begins to shake you, remember what God has done in the past. Express your confidence that He has a plan and a purpose in your life. You are not a quitter; you are a conqueror through the work Jesus did on the cross. Stop focusing on what you can't do, and remember that nothing is too hard for God.

Nothing.

3

Right Where You Are

Do what you can, with what you've got, where you are.
—A FRIEND OF THEODORE ROOSEVELT

W hat's the first thing that pops into your head when I mention the words *mission-possible life*? Do you think of a preacher sharing about Jesus? Or how about a missionary choosing to live in a remote village without Wi-Fi or indoor plumbing to share the gospel with people from other parts of the world? On one hand, yes, those are certainly mission-possible vocations. On the other hand, living out a mission is more holistic and less dramatic than you might imagine.

Being a mission-possible Christian has less to do with being a "professional Christian" and more to do with developing an intimate relationship with Jesus. Mission stems from embracing our identity in Him. When we deepen our walk with Jesus, He invades every part of our lives. He doesn't become real only at a church service, youth group, or worship event. We represent Him all the time, everywhere we go: at school, at practice, and at home.

Whatever you are tasked with in the everyday—even what you believe are the most trivial duties—find a way to invite purpose into that space. What can you do to make someone's life better after he or she has interacted with you? Knowing God is on your side, how can you approach a challenge you've been avoiding? Whether you're dealing with annoying younger siblings or trying to balance homework, soccer, and a million chores, think about what you could be doing differently to tell the story that you belong to God.

To the Miss Nancys of the World

The church I attended growing up was known for its theatrical productions of faith-based musicals. We're talking as "big and wow" as Broadway. Hundreds of people in the cast. A full orchestra. Live animals. Incredible sets and costumes. Thousands would attend, and even more would tune in when performances were broadcast on television.

I loved watching these plays, but I never wanted to be in them. I wasn't comfortable speaking in public. It wasn't that I hated it—I just didn't feel confident. My parents took notice of this early on and did what good parents do: They made me do it. They signed me up for any activity in which I needed to stand in front of a crowd and talk, even sing. That's right, sing. Mom and Dad made me pray out loud in front of others. They forced me to give presentations at science fairs. And then they encouraged me to do my favorite thing in the world as a kid (note my sarcasm): audition for church plays. It was the worst. I would much rather have done a hundred push-ups than sung a song to showcase my skills for a part in a play about Noah.

I remember one of my first auditions. Eight-year-old Tim Tebow stood on the center of a huge platform, staring into the eyes of multiple judges and a few others who were seated in the grand auditorium. The judges, void of facial expression, were ready to assess if I was worthy of being cast in the play. Like the rest of the candidates, I was supposed to introduce my performance by stating my name, my age, my grade, and a favorite quote, such as a Bible verse. Can't really screw that up, right? I said my name but forgot to mention my age and grade because I was so nervous.

The second I cleared my throat and heard the scratchy sound blast through the microphone, my body began to tremble. Eyes fixed on my feet, I mumbled some poem my parents made me memorize—that was my quote. I don't know if the judges could even hear or understand a word I said. Staring down at my shoelaces, I gulped a deep breath, trying to psych myself up for the next worst thing: I had to sing. There's a good reason I was on *Lip Sync Battle* and not *American Idol*. It's not a talent God gifted me with. Dying for this moment of humiliation to end, I rushed through "Jesus Loves Me," which I chose because it was the easiest song I could remember. Every sound that leaped from my throat fumbled out of pitch. When I was done squawking the last line, I speed-walked to the side curtain. Relief swept over me. Though I'd been uncomfortable every second of standing on that stage, I was proud I had done it.

Somehow I got a part in the play. I was chosen to play a camel's butt. Let that sink in for a minute.

About that time, I was finally old enough to sign up for the church choir. Obviously, Mom and Dad were delighted. I definitely did not share their enthusiasm. But then I met my choir teacher, Miss Nancy. She left such a positive lasting impression on me as a kid that I was honored to be able to invite her to my wedding about two decades later. To this day, whenever I think about her or mention her name, I can't help but smile and feel grateful.

Miss Nancy was my choir teacher from second grade through fifth. She guided me from my humble beginnings as a camel's butt to performing in my last couple of elementary school plays as a Supreme Court justice and Superman. That's quite an impressive progression over a few years.

I may have been basically taking up space in choir due to my lack of talent, but I was happy to do my best for this special teacher. Miss Nancy had a gift. It wasn't just that she was a great teacher who had remarkable musical talent. She was passionate about her work. She used her position and talents to make a difference. She cared about the students. And she made every one of us feel special, even the kids like me who couldn't carry a tune past the first three notes.

What I especially loved about Miss Nancy was how she flipped what I had considered awful into something fun. It wasn't her skill that made this happen; it was how she taught from the heart.

Miss Nancy's spirit was full of joy. It showed in the smile that always glowed on her face, her positive attitude, and her words of encouragement to all her students, both the ones who had talent and the ones who were better at other things. Even the teachers who worked with her, like Miss Tammy, shared her passion. Let me be clear that my dislike of choir and singing didn't change. If I could sing, I would have loved it, but I sucked. It was my admiration for Miss Nancy and her team that made me want to do more than just stand there and mouth some lyrics. My teacher created an environment that grew musical gifts and drew out the best in her students. It's what I saw her do with excellence, and it's what made me consider her one of my favorites.

Unlike some teachers, Miss Nancy didn't see me as a one-sided jock or give me a hard time when I had to miss a rehearsal because I had a game. To me that was a huge deal. I can't tell you how many times teachers and even leaders at church would roll their eyes or make some snide remark because I'd miss or be late to a service or an event because of sports. Not Miss Nancy. Sometimes she'd even let me get a rehearsal in before a game or practice. And she always asked how my sporting event went. That's genuine care right there, and it's something I'll never forget. I may not have shown a shred of theatrical stardom, but I truly enjoyed the plays she put on twice a year—so much so that when I got older, I invited the teammates on my travel team to see the productions. A few of them even made the decision to trust in Jesus because of these events! This never would have happened if it weren't for Miss Nancy.

I was so influenced by Miss Nancy's passion and her mission-possible life that right after I won the Heisman, I came back to play Goliath in one of her plays. That's how much I respected and appreciated my teacher. And if she asked me to sing for her today, I'd grab a mic and belt out whatever she wanted, no doubt.

The Miss Nancys of the world bless our lives. They say or do things we'll never forget. But they're not just teachers. They're the moms and dads who hug their kids close and cry with them when Mufasa dies in *The Lion King*. They're the kids who stick up for the ones who are being bullied. They're the boys and girls who bring encouragement instead of complaints. They're the ones who say "I'll try" instead of "It can't be done." You don't have to teach a music class to be a Miss Nancy; you just have to be willing to notice others and treat them as Jesus would treat you.

Whatever You Do

As I look back at the life of Jesus, I realize something: He lived each day present and aware and fueled by intentional action. Wherever He went, His purpose didn't stop, even when He spent time alone to pray. He forgave those who were shamed. He fed those who were hungry. He paid attention to those who had been forgotten or ignored. He loved the last, the least, and the lost. Those are things we all can do no matter how old or young we are or how many followers we have on social media.

It's about honoring God in everything we do. The Bible teaches this very principle. Ecclesiastes 9:10 tells us, "Whatever your hand finds to do, do it with all your might." The apostle Paul, who was known for his devotion to Christ and his positive attitude even in the worst of circumstances, wrote, "Whether you eat or drink, or whatever you do, do all things for the glory of God" (1 Corinthians 10:31).

He gave the same directive in the third chapter of Colossians:

Whatever you do in word or deed, do everything in the name of the Lord Jesus, giving thanks through Him to God the Father. . . . Whatever you do, do your work heartily, as for the Lord and not for people, knowing that it is from the Lord that you will receive the reward of the inheritance. It is the Lord Christ whom you serve. (verses 17, 23–24)

In these passages, Paul is giving Christians a genuine command. What he's saying is, "May all your actions, no matter what, whether you're studying, practicing, or hanging out with friends, reflect a heart that loves Jesus."

Whatever you do, do it with all your might. If you don't, you are not valuing the time God gives you. You're telling Him that His gift is not worth it. You may not be happy with where you are, but He can still pull purpose through it. You can have ambition to be somewhere better or do something else and strive toward those things, but never forget that God can and will use you wherever you are in the process.

Purpose is intertwined in every area of your life. Besides my relationships with God and Demi, TTF is the most important thing in my life because I want to bring faith, hope, and love to the world. But guess what? I still speak for many other nonprofit organizations. My purpose doesn't have borders. Even though I can't share the gospel while working on *SEC Nation* or *First Take*, I can still have joy and passion and purpose in what I do and ask people how they are and genuinely care about their answers. I can still reflect the love of God to others in how I act and treat people.

There's power in allowing God to manifest His presence in whatever you do, right here and right now. One way to do this is to take pride in all the work you do, whether you're cleaning your room for the umpteenth time or studying for an algebra exam.

Mission Excellence

In 605 B.C., King Nebuchadnezzar of the Babylonian Empire had invaded Israel and taken captive many of its men, women, and children. It would be seventy years before these kidnapped people would return to their homeland.

A guy named Daniel and three of his buddies were among the people chosen for a specialized government training program. They were smart, good looking, strong, and young, likely between the ages of eleven and eighteen. But this opportunity came with some serious drawbacks. Sure, they weren't handcuffed or thrown into a dirty prison cell without food or water. Still, they were captives, and not a day went by when they weren't reminded of this bleak reality.

But Daniel's captivity was also an opportunity. Another prophet, by the name of Jeremiah, had prophesied this very event. Jeremiah also gave some encouragement the exiles could lean into. "Build houses and live in them; and plant gardens and eat their produce. . . . Seek the prosperity of the city where I have sent you into exile, and pray to the LORD in its behalf; for in its prosperity will be your prosperity" (Jeremiah 29:5, 7). In other words, make yourselves at home, because you're going to be here for a while.

So Daniel transformed a kidnapping into a mission. He had been handpicked for this three-year training program that would make him and his friends into diplomats of sorts who would one day serve the nation of Babylon. Daniel learned the Babylonian language and was educated in their history, customs, and culture. He was obedient throughout his forced service, but he never forgot his spiritual heritage.

Daniel was one of three who were appointed to oversee 120 satraps, chief representatives of the king. He was good at his job. really good. The Bible tells us, "This Daniel began distinguishing himself among the commissioners and satraps because he possessed an extraordinary spirit, and the king intended to appoint him over the entire kingdom" (Daniel 6:3). Wow! The king was going to give Daniel the keys to the Babylonian kingdom.

As Daniel proved himself an excellent leader, those around him started turning an ugly shade of green. How could this lowly Israelite sprint up the ladder so fast and be charged with such authority and power? It wasn't fair. And it was quite a blow to their egos. So these men thought up a scheme that would surely burst their colleague's happy bubble (insert evil laughter). They hired top-notch investigators to find and expose the skeletons in Daniel's closet. But there was no dirt to be found, not even a hint of indiscretion. "And no negligence or corruption was to be found in him" (verse 4).

We can learn a lot from the life of Daniel. He fought for excellence. He worked and studied and trained hard. He went the extra mile. He showed up early and stayed late. He wasn't satisfied to just get by. He wanted to do more. This pursuit was inherent in his spirit. It was part of his DNA. He was a great illustration of Ecclesiastes 9:10.

I love the SEC slogan "It just means more." It reminds me of how Daniel lived his life. Miss Nancy too. A job wasn't just a job. For these two people, their employment meant more than just getting a pat on the back or a good grade. They transcended their roles in ways that brought joy and purpose to their lives and the lives of others.

Living a mission-possible life means watering and fertilizing and cultivating the ground where you are planted, even if it seems nothing more than a wasteland. I love what Jesus said in Luke 16:10: "The one who is faithful in a very little thing is also faithful in much; and the one who is unrighteous in a very little thing is also unrighteous in much." I try to look for such faithfulness in the people who work with me. If I see someone who is faithful and doing a great job with smaller assignments, I take notice.

The way I see it, there are three practical ways to live a mission-possible life with the excellence that Daniel modeled for us.

1. Act with Integrity, Even If No One Is Watching

As I was growing up, my parents created a rewards program for us five kids called Daddy's Dollars. Every time someone outside our family complimented our character, Dad would give us a dollar. Sometimes he'd give us a real bill, other times a printed paper we could exchange for a prize in a chest of goodies or for privileges, such as TV or computer time. We would also get dollars for doing extra chores. My family is extremely competitive. It didn't matter if we were playing Monopoly or basketball—we would hustle and duke it out and do everything in our power to win. Even as the youngest of five, I was determined to get the most Daddy's Dollars out of everyone, so I worked hard for compliments. I helped carry groceries. I always held the door open for someone. I was first to raise my hand to volunteer. And I did most of these things in front of my parents, on purpose, so they could see how awesome I was and give me a buck. And that was the problem.

Eventually, I realized how empty it was to do nice things for a dollar or a pat on the back or any other material reward. I remembered one of the Bible verses I memorized growing up: "The ways of everyone are before the eyes of the LORD, and He observes all his paths" (Proverbs 5:21). God is always watching us. He sees us doing the right thing, the wrong thing, and nothing. Who are you when no one is watching? Do you do the right thing because it's simply the right thing to do? When we start living and acting as though God's eyes are always watching, we will start living a little differently. And even if no one notices that you helped the new kid find his way around school or were kind to your little sister yesterday, it doesn't matter. While it's nice to be rewarded with stuff, it's more fulfilling to please our heavenly Father.

2. Have a Heart of Gratitude

There were many times as a professional athlete when I wasn't crazy about an outcome. Getting cut, for instance. It stung every time. And although I was crazy blessed outside of football, it was easy to feel bitter at not getting something I'd worked so hard for. I've learned the importance of flipping my mentality and choosing gratitude every time. That's not easy to do when we find ourselves in a funk or grumpy for what we may think is a pretty good reason.

I don't know about you, but for me it can happen every now and then in a split second on an ordinary Sunday afternoon. I could have had a super spiritual morning at church, fun time with family and friends at brunch, but then, while watching a quarterback play in an NFL game and listening to announcers make a passing comment about something he may not have done so well, get a little twisted thinking about how those same commentators would have said some nasty things about me on the same play. And all of a sudden I forget about the great worship experience from a few hours earlier or how good I felt hanging with my mom and munching on delicious steak. I sulk, and if I refuse to do anything about it, I stay stuck in that ugly place. I have to be mindful of what I'm feeling. I have to think about what I'm thinking about. And I have to choose to think about what God has done in my life and how faithful He is. It may take time to remedy my poor attitude, but I commit to choosing thankfulness. It's funny what happens when I shift to being grateful. Everything changes. I find myself smiling more. The muscles in my neck relax, and the headache I had goes away. I don't snap at people. I act more loving with my wife. And then I'm in a much better mood (though I still disagree with the critics).

There's a lot to be said for the regular practice of gratitude. The benefits are many. For one, being grateful improves a person's physical health. A study conducted by psychologists at the University of Miami observed a group of subjects. A third of them were asked to keep a daily journal of all the things that happened that they were grateful for. Another third of the subjects were asked to write down the events that happened that irritated them. The final group of subjects were asked to record daily events without specifically either a positive or negative description. At the end of the ten-week study, in comparison to the other two groups, the group that practiced gratitude felt more optimistic and positive about life, were more physically active, and had fewer visits to the doctor.[1] There are many studies that include similar findings. Gratitude improves relationships, produces better moods, and is good for your health. You may not feel like it, but there's always a reason to be grateful. Even right now, thank God for the very breath you are breathing and His presence that is within you this very moment.

3. Do Everything with Excellence

Aim to be and even top your personal best. Whether you're a barista, a grocery bagger, or a babysitter, do your job with excellence. Make an effort. Put in the work.

Your Work Is Worship

The Hebrew word *avad* is used to express the English concepts of work, worship, and service. A mission-possible life must be shaped by *avad*. God has integrated our relationships with Him into the everyday. Our faith walks affect everything we do. We worship God when we spend time with our family. We worship Him when we practice our soccer drills. We worship Him when we study our history notes one last time. Living a mission-possible life, in whatever our hands find to do, is an act of worship. Even if we feel we have little to offer in terms of money or talent, we are mission forward when we choose to use what we have to glorify God. In 1 Corinthians 3:9, Paul reminds us that "we are God's fellow workers."

I recently received a beautiful letter from a seventeen-year-old girl named Fiorella Siu. She lives in El Salvador, a country she noted is the smallest in Central America. Even before I continued to read the letter, that intentional detail reminded me of the story of Gideon in the Bible. God called Gideon a "valiant warrior" (Judges 6:12) and commanded him to rise up and save the nation of Israel. Gideon refused at first, offering what he felt was a legitimate excuse: "O Lord, how am I to save Israel? Behold, my family is the least in Manasseh, and I am the youngest in my father's house" (verse 15). I've learned that God can do a lot with our little. If we hold on to what we have, that's all we have. But if we give God even things we consider insignificant, He will not only receive them but also multiply them.

Fiorella knows what it's like to suffer: from developing symptoms that mirrored the signs of leukemia but ultimately being healed in her body to witnessing firsthand her parents' financial devastation when she was ten years old and remembering what it was like to stand in a grocery store with only a dollar in her hand. But these struggles didn't harden her spirit; they strengthened her dependence on God and shaped her heart to beat toward others. Knowing how it felt to want, her parents always encouraged her to help others, to share food when someone is hungry, and to show God's love when someone feels lost or afraid.

Fiorella wrote,

I've always felt like I can't fit in with the youth of nowadays, but now my way of looking at things is different. I've always had this urge to evangelize and show God's love for others, but sometimes I feel like I'm not old enough or don't have enough money to make an impact in this world.

I've finally understood that my life is not always going to be about myself. God has chosen me to make a difference. What really matters is how I live to help others and show His love through the small acts I can do.

As a family, we pray for God's blessing so that we can bless others. I no longer care about the material things or how successful I can be on earth but on the souls I impact by sharing God's love. The most important thing I can do is reflect Jesus's attributes so that other people can experience how important they are to God. When I realized that I wanted to reflect Jesus, my way of viewing things and interacting with others, even with my family, changed. Now I'm more aware of how I speak and how I treat others. Now I'd rather care about what God thinks of me than what others will. I'd rather be criticized for being "weird" than disappoint God for trying to fit in with the crowd.

From now on, I want to put others' lives and needs

above my own. I really want to be remembered as a symbol of God's love to others. I know that God will see my heart and desires and that He can use them to make miracles like He used the five loaves of bread and two fish of a little young man to feed thousands.

Fiorella, I have a pretty good feeling that God sees your heart and is so proud of you!

We may feel insignificant or unseen, or we may think our talents pale in comparison to what we see on TV or social media, but when we offer God our willingness in everything we do, we position ourselves for miracles, for eternal impact, and for increasing a spiritual legacy no one can take away. When our lives are immersed in *avad*—like the lives of Miss Nancy, Daniel, and Fiorella—we will have opportunities to grow and to live out our missions.

Never underestimate what God can do when you offer what you have and who you are fully to Him. It's not your stuff He wants or needs; it's your willingness to live your life—every part of it—for Him.

4

Mission-Possible Superpowers

The pursuit of God is not a part-time, weekend
exercise.... It is a pursuit of passion.
—R. C. SPROUL

M y father has done and said many things that have made
me a better man. I'll never forget what he did for me when
I was eight years old. Though it shocked me then, over the years it
has revolutionized my definition of *passion*.

At the time, my father had spent a few months serving in the
Philippines while Mom was at home in Jacksonville, Florida, taking care of us five kids. We missed him terribly. The day he arrived
back in the States was like Christmas, even without the sparkling
lights and red-and-green overload. When we saw Dad coming
toward us in the airport, we bolted toward him. Each of us kids
grabbed some part of him and hung on for dear life.

Dad drove us home from the airport. Before we got to the farm
where we lived, he made a stop at Blockbuster. (In case you've

never heard of it before, it was a store where we used to rent movies before we could stream them online. Yeah, that was a thing.) He didn't tell us what movie he rented; he said it was a surprise.

After we got home and gave Dad a chance to settle in, he called out for me and my two older brothers to meet him in the family room. I can't remember if he told us what the movie was about before he hit play, but he did set it up with a moving speech that echoes in my ears today.

As Dad spoke to us, tears flooded his face. I don't remember exactly what he said, but he definitely had our undivided attention. To the best of my memory, it went something like this:

I just want you to know how much I love you and how proud I am of you and how much I believe in you. I know that all of you are ambitious and you want to accomplish things in your life. It's my job as your dad to give you an edge, to give you an advantage, so that you're not like every other person and so you remember that you are unique. In a moment, I'm going to hit play on this movie. And first, I want you to watch it and really study it, especially the main character. Because, boys, if you love whatever it is that you want to do, like the man you're going to see in this movie, you will be different. You will be special.

He took a breath and continued,

Second, I want you to have passion like this man for whatever it is that you want to do. Third, I want you to be willing to sacrifice, because if you're willing to love what you do, be passionate about it, and be willing to sacrifice for whatever it is, you're going to be different. You're going to be contagious. You're going to be special, and people are going to want to be around you.

Then he pressed play and sat down on the couch next to Mom. Obviously, I didn't know the man he was referring to in the movie (which, by the way, Dad had just watched on the plane ride back home), but his name was spoken in the first minute of the opening scene. That scene begins innocently enough with the droning melody of bagpipes serenading dreamy shots of rugged mountains and a misty sky, but it gives way to a young William Wallace witnessing the aftermath of a massacre. Yeah, I wasn't quite prepared for that. I'm talking about *Braveheart*, the epic historical-fiction account of the legendary Wallace, one of Scotland's historical national heroes.

Braveheart tells the story of a Scottish warrior who rallies his countrymen in the late 1200s against the brutal British monarch who rules Scotland. His mission is to lead his country to freedom so his people can live free from British tyranny. The road to freedom was paved with sacrifice and ultimately required Wallace to pay with his life.

An eight-year-old watching *Braveheart* was a little intense. No doubt my mom was absolutely mortified. Aside from the fact that it features many gory battle scenes, there were a few parts that showed mild nudity. Like a good mother, she tried her best to cover our eyes during those parts. In Dad's defense, he'd watched the edited airplane version, so many of the scenes were a bit of a surprise to him too. Now, considering I was young when I watched the movie for the first time, I wasn't really prepared to process all the complicated themes the film portrayed, but Dad got his point across. I wanted to live with fierce courage and passion like Wallace.

As I got older and rewatched the film many times, I began to understand its underlying themes of conviction and perseverance. And I truly soaked in the wisdom Dad imparted to us through this film.

Passion Meets Purpose

That *Braveheart* viewing wasn't the only time my dad taught us the importance of passion for a cause. He'd repeat the same message many times over the years: when he'd drop me off for church events, sports practices, and games, and when we'd toss the ball around in the yard. "Love what you do," he'd tell me. "Be passionate about it. It's so important that you go after what you really love to do and that it matters."

I like to think of passion as a superpower.

Most superheroes have special abilities that help them withstand challenges and overcome obstacles. These superpowers set them apart from mere mortals as well as their enemies. Take the world's most recognizable superhero, Superman. His core superpowers include flight, speed, strength, and X-ray vision. As familiar a character as he is to most of us, he has some superhero characteristics that are not commonly known. For instance, he can clone himself. In one episode, he is depicted as being in two places at once to save Lois Lane. He is also a super kisser. He smooched Lois so passionately one particular time that he wiped out her memory. She couldn't remember that Clark Kent and Superman were the same person. I guess the writers meant that to be sweet at the time, but it's a little creepy in hindsight.

When it comes to purpose, many of us are drawn to certain characteristics we believe are necessary, like talent or skill or platform. But there are requirements to living a mission-possible life that may not be so obvious. I believe one of those is passion.

We think of passion today as an intense desire, often a romantic one. We think we see it when a man pursues a woman (or vice versa). He is so in love with her that he does everything in his power to win her heart. He writes her schmaltzy love songs. He buys her elaborate gifts. He is relentless in his pursuit. But the word *passion* used to mean a whole lot more.

Passion is deeper than feeling excited or being hyped up. It's got more layers than a fickle emotion. The word *passion* comes from the Latin *pati*, "to suffer." I don't know anyone who would pick the word *suffer* as a synonym for *passion*. The Latin word for passion was first used to describe the death of Jesus. His arrest, subsequent torture, and death by crucifixion are the events sometimes referred to as Passion narratives. So, it turns out that the true story of passion is a story about suffering.

If you want to have the passion that fuels a mission-possible life, do something that you are willing to suffer for. Hold up! I know that sounds crazy. Stay with me. It's not about torturing yourself for a greater cause; it's about being willing to stick it out and fight for what you believe in when the glitz and glamour vanish and no one is watching.

While Chad Hymas was building his elk farm in Utah, he broke his neck in a freak accident that left him paraplegic at twenty-seven years old. As he recovered from his injury and introduced his new body to his old life, he wanted to achieve a goal most people would think was impossible. He refused to allow his paralysis to limit his experiences, so he began to build bigger expectations for himself.

Two years later, in 2003, he logged 513 miles in 104 hours over 11 days by pushing himself in a three-wheeled bike from downtown Salt Lake City to Las Vegas. It's roughly a 6.5-hour car ride. I read Chad's story in the book *Aspire: Discovering Your Purpose Through the Power of Words*, written by Kevin Hall, who accompanied Chad on part of his adventure. Kevin describes how, at the beginning of this journey, there were police escorts, large cheering crowds, and cameras from many different media outlets recording this remarkable and inspirational journey. Everyone was watching and cheering Chad on.

Then came the darker part: "It wouldn't be until later, when the TV lights and police escorts were long gone, when there was no one on the curb to applaud and encourage, when the road turned upward, when his arms ached, when he was tired and hungry, that it would get difficult."[1] But even when the excitement faded, Chad was willing to suffer for his passion. He saw the other side of being weary. He could have easily decided to give up after such a severe injury, but he had a passion to make a difference through his suffering and beyond his pain.

When you get tired, true passion is what will see you through. When no one is around to help boost your confidence, passion will help you take the next step. When you get stuck or hit a wall, passion will give you momentum to recover and press forward. In your desire to live armed with purpose, find out where your passions lie. What are you willing to stand up for in the face of challenge? What are you willing to achieve no matter the cost? You might know exactly where your passion lies, or maybe you're not so sure. Here are a few questions to help shed some light:

1. *What do you enjoy doing?* What do you look forward to doing that fires you up? Volunteering at a local animal shelter? Helping people? Babysitting?

2. *Whom do you want to help the most?* Is your heart moved with compassion toward those with learning disabilities? Or the elderly?

3. *What problem do you want to help solve?* Do you care about people having clean water? Are you drawn to providing nutrition to those who live in food-insecure homes?

4. *Are there any themes in what you read, listen to, talk about, and research?* Think about all you do in a day, the shows you watch, the books you read, and your Googling habits. Can you see any common threads?

When you're thick in the process of discovering your passion, remind yourself that each person's journey is unique. Don't look to your best friend or sibling to determine what you choose to fight for. You are one of one. You were not created to be a replica of anyone else. Find the passion that beats to the rhythm of your own heart.

Find and Use Your Edge

There's something about having to do more with less as I grew up that developed in me an inner drive, or what I like to call an edge. My parents didn't have a lot of money when they were raising us kids. We didn't wear designer clothes or go on fancy vacations. But Mom and Dad taught us the value of a dollar and the blessing of hard work. They instilled in us a work ethic I nurture to this day, as well as an inner drive that feeds my desire to pursue my dreams and strive to be the best at whatever I'm doing.

"Anyone want a Gatorade?" I can't tell you how many times I heard those words playing sports as a kid. Every little hand would shoot up except mine. "No thanks. I've got water," I'd say. It wasn't that I didn't like Gatorade. Of course I did! But I also knew that it was a lot more expensive than good ol' H_2O (and not the bottled kind—the kind that gushed from a tap into a reusable bottle). Mom and Dad were missionaries. Living on a limited income taught them to be frugal, and that meant Gatorade wasn't on our grocery list. It also meant that going out to lunch after church on Sundays wasn't a recurring event and that the only time we'd be able to enjoy a snow cone after games was when our team would win, because then the cones were free.

My parents' intentional financial practices also gave us kids room to contribute to our family. Mom and Dad were definitely equal-opportunity employers. Growing up on a farm, we had all the fruits and vegetables we wanted and then some. We ate a lot of what we helped grow and sold the rest. Sell what you sow, right?

When I was in Little League, every now and then in between games and practices, I'd grab whatever basket of fresh vegetables Mom or Dad had brought that day and walk around the stands selling what I could. This may have impressed the parents a bit, but the kids got quite a kick out of it. I'd get made fun of. A lot. Whatever. I never let the sneers or jabs bother me. I was a confident kid and able to pull off selling cucumbers, squash, and zucchini as if it were something any cool kid would do.

I've never gotten a trophy for gardening, but I've learned a few things from years of picking the fruits of our labor on our farm. The most practical lesson I learned was to wear gloves and long sleeves, as some fruits and vegetables are more aggressive than others. Take okra, for instance. This slimy fruit is covered in tiny spines that can easily prick and itch your skin. Pitching with okra hands is not fun.

As I learned to take care of my hands, my parents also taught me how to take care of all the other stuff the good Lord had given me. In the context of Little League, this meant my bat. I remember the first new one my parents ever gave me. It was a Redline. And the first time I used it, I hit a home run off the very first pitch. Many of my teammates were going through two or three bats a season. I was the kid who always had to borrow a bat or use the team's equipment. Having my own bat—one that had never been used before—filled me with a great sense of pride. I handled the bat with care when it wasn't swinging in my hands. I knew how hard my parents had worked to honor me with my own bat, and I didn't want to take that for granted. I used that bat for years—the same one, every game, every practice.

Watching my parents stretch a dollar and hustling as many cucumbers as I could impressed upon me the truth that even the most expensive glove or the best cleats aren't going to magically make you faster or stronger. But an edge will. *Edge* can be defined as "an improved position or advantage." I consider edge to be an intestinal fortitude that stems from our passion, grows from our experiences (positive or negative), and fires up in the face of opposition.

I used my family's financial situation to find my edge. Dad may not have been able to get me the latest Jordans, but he'd spray-paint the driveway so I could run drills. He may not have been able to afford to buy me a gym membership, but he took the time to weld together whatever weights he could find so I could get in a good workout. He also built my brothers and me a batting cage made out of wood and fishing nets and would throw to us for hours and hours when he wasn't abroad. I'll never forget the day football face masks went on sale at a local sporting goods store. All the good athletes had one, except me. They were too expensive. Mom was so excited when she found one we could afford, except it was the wrong color. That afternoon, Mom and I spent time together, kneeling over a floor of newspapers we had put down to spray-paint my helmet the color of our team. It felt amazing to finally have a face mask like the other kids. Even so, my confidence came not from the painted mask but from the edge my parents instilled in me as we made it.

I chose not to perceive what my parents couldn't give me as a disadvantage, but rather as an opportunity to strengthen my natural abilities. I put in longer hours, trained harder, and stepped it up when it stopped feeling fun. The kids would make fun of my beat-up or too-big hand-me-down gear at the start of each season, but I used that mockery to stir in me a passion to put in the extra work. I may not have had a gym membership, but I had a hard-work membership. My mentality, even as a kid, was "I may not be wearing the most expensive cleats, but I'm going to be the fastest and strongest member on this team."

I truly believe that having the same financial advantages other kids had would not have served me the same way. I wouldn't have gained the edge that I nurtured as I got older and even after I could afford the fancy cleats. In a way, this fortitude looked like a chip—no, a boulder—on my shoulder. And I used it to my advantage. I knew how hard my parents worked, and I believed in them and wanted to honor them by pushing my limits physically. If I ever have children one day, I pray I can give them that same loving support I received and help shape for them an edge that money can't buy.

Find your edge and use it. It'll take you beyond what you imagine are your limits.

Having an edge doesn't mean you'll meet all your goals and accomplish every single thing you set out to achieve, but it gives you the best chance at being different. As Dad said, we don't have to be like everyone else. We can set ourselves apart in a good way. We can do it our way, equipped and empowered not by human strength or skill but by the Spirit of God living within us. You may not strive to be an athlete, but you can have an edge because God has called you to be different. Your perfect is yours alone. When society tells you that you have to be this or wear that or say this or do that, you can have the confidence to withstand that pressure and pursue your mission and live life God's way.

What's your superhero edge? Before you start thinking of what you are not or what you don't have, think of what you've gained from your experiences. What have you overcome? What do you know more of now because of what you have been through yesterday?

My experiences growing up helped me find my edge, but mostly I have an edge because I believe in God and because He has been and will be faithful. The more you fall in love with Jesus, and the more you understand the edge He gives you, the more you are willing to go out on a limb and even suffer for something you believe in. Ultimately, for each believer, that sacrifice, that passion, is what it means to win the race of faith.

5

Purpose in the Present

The great doesn't happen through impulse alone, and is
a succession of little things that are brought together.
—VINCENT VAN GOGH

'll never forget the first time the idea of hosting proms for kids
with special needs, which has come to be known as Night to
Shine, came about. I was talking to the director of the foundation
at the time about our upcoming fifth anniversary.

He mentioned he knew of two churches in the country that
were hosting dances for people with developmental disabilities.
"Since you and the foundation love people with special needs,
would you want to do something like that to celebrate our five-
year anniversary?"

"Absolutely!"

"Awesome! So right here in Jacksonville?"

I didn't have to think twice. "Everywhere. I'd like to host these
events all around the world!"

He looked at me like I had sprouted four extra heads. "No, seriously."

"I *am* serious." From what I'd heard about what these dances had looked like, plus what I'd seen over the years of how poorly people with special needs are treated, especially in some countries where they are discounted as human beings and even thrown away in the trash, I knew I wanted to take this celebration worldwide. I had big dreams in that moment (not that I knew how to execute them or even where to start). The only thing I did know was that God loves each and every one of us.

I didn't want to just host a cool event; I wanted to offer an experience guests would never forget. But it wouldn't be about the glitz and glamour of an amazing night of dancing and fun. That stuff is good and makes people smile, but it's the love of God that changes hearts and souls. And in my mind, that's what the event was about. Not a party, but a showering of God's love.

As we started quickly moving toward making this event a reality, many people around us had questions, even a few folks who were really close to our team. I'll be the first to admit that I totally get why they were asking them. And as this was the first time we were doing something like this, I may not have had the best answers to the questions.

But I couldn't shake the feeling that we needed to passionately pursue this dream. And in this instance, all the questions seemed to take away from the vision. I knew I had to listen to the pull of my heart, and I believed that this idea was aligned with Scripture. The more conversations our team had about it and the more pushback we faced, the more my faith grew and the more I knew that having this event felt right. That said, I didn't know exactly how or if it would work, but I just wanted to help people feel loved, and this was a channel to help make that happen. See, my mission was never to put on Night to Shine. Now, I love it and it's absolutely my favorite night of the year, but my mission has always been to love, celebrate, and care for those God loves, celebrates, and cares for. Night to Shine was one way to accomplish this mission.

Have you ever avoided doing something because you didn't have all the answers? Has your idea ever fallen flat because you got hung up on having everything figured out? Even when we want to pursue what we feel is the right thing, our passion can start to fade if God doesn't show up in our dreams with a step-by-step blueprint for *how* and *where* and *why* everything is going to work out. Why is it that when we don't have *all* the information, we tend to do nothing?

Pursue the *What,* and God Will Take Care of the *Why* and *How*

I know what it's like to pray and ask God for guidance in making a decision and not hear a clear response. I've often prayed and asked the Lord to show me the answer. I sought wise counsel, I talked to pastors, but I still felt stuck. And you know what? Not hearing specific guidance or direction doesn't mean God isn't leading me, nor does it mean He is not with me.

Part of walking by faith and not by sight (see 2 Corinthians 5:7) is that sometimes we just don't know what God wants us to do.

We may believe we have a sense of where He is leading us, but often He doesn't leak the details.

If you look through the Bible, you'll notice that God has a habit of handing out assignments in which He reveals the *what* (and sometimes not too much of that) and very little of the *how* and *why*. It seems like He's always giving us opportunities to depend on Him rather than ourselves.

You might remember the story of Noah and the ark in Genesis 6 and 7. God had an unusual mission for Noah. Not only was this mission something that hadn't been done before, but it was also going to take a crazy amount of time and seem ludicrous.

"There's going to be a flood, so build a gigantic boat for me to save you and your family," God basically told Noah and then proceeded to give him detailed instructions on how to do it. Here's the kicker. There is no mention of *falling* rain in the Bible before the flood. The earth, according to some scholars, may have been watered by only a mist. Others believe the amount of water in the ground was enough to hydrate the earth's vegetation or that humans may have created a type of irrigation system. In any case, no one could have anticipated a violent rainstorm, let alone a flood.

It could have taken Noah close to a hundred years to build this massive ship. A hundred years! I waited a long time to meet the right woman, but I don't know if I could have waited another seventy or eighty years. (Who are we kidding? For Demi? Of course I would have!)

Noah must have been exhausted after almost a century of

measuring, cutting, and hammering all day. Picture with me what it must have felt like to be him.

Noah lets out a big sigh and settles onto the gopher-wood floor. He smiles, beaming proudly at the smooth surface. Not a bad sanding job for a first-timer. Biting into his peanut-butter-and-jelly sandwich, he tries to ignore his bickering coworkers: his three sons. It is only day thirty, and the framework built barely resembles the skeleton of a massive ship. But it is something that wasn't there thirty days ago.

Noah's day will be over soon and he'll be home taking a long hot bath. He dreads the comments that await him on social media.

"An ark? He's got nothing better to do? Why doesn't he get a real job?"

"God spoke to him? really? What makes him so special?"

"He must have gotten a good sponsorship deal with the construction tools or something."

Noah keeps any doubts that creep up to himself. And although he doesn't totally agree with those negative opinions of his project, he can't ignore that dull gnawing in his spirit: *Is this some sort of sick joke or twisted test? How much longer can I keep up this grueling pace? Will rain really come? This doesn't make sense. None of it does!*

As he chews and questions and contemplates his mission, he sighs. What else is he going to do? So after flicking off the crumbs stuck on his beard, he picks up his hammer and keeps going. *Bam, bam, bam!*

One day, shortly after turning six hundred years old, Noah notices the sky mysteriously darken well before sunset. Lightning cracks in the distance. And out of nowhere, a blanket of angry clouds begins to shroud every inch of daylight, the overture to an outpouring of rain pelting the ground. Noah and his family take cover in the ark. As rolling thunder shakes the ship, Noah remembers what God told him: "After seven more days, I will send rain on the earth for forty days and forty nights" (Genesis 7:4). Almost a century has passed since Noah had received God's mission command.

What can we learn from this man who had stayed faithful even in the face of many questions and doubts? It's not about knowing every detail or having an answer for every question; it's about stepping out in faith and doing what you know is the right thing to do, the thing that God wants you to do. If it's starting a Bible study at school, you do it. If it's inviting the kid no one talks to out to lunch, you do it. If it's helping your elderly neighbor carry groceries, you do it.

You move forward in your mission even if you make a mistake or take a wrong turn. Let's park here for a sec. Mission-possible living is not about perfection; it's about a person, and that person is Jesus. Walking by faith isn't about never messing up; it's about admitting that you are made righteous because you've placed your trust in Jesus. If you find yourself off track because you made the wrong decision or stumbled along the way, don't focus on that mistake. There will never be a day in which we make perfect choices, have perfect thoughts, and make all the right moves. I'm so glad imperfections don't disqualify us from finishing the race.

The only thing that keeps us from moving mission forward is

ourselves. We are responsible for keeping it moving, even if it's taking us longer than expected, even when our friends think we're crazy, and even if others question our motives. When you don't know what to do, depend on God. You don't need to have it all figured out. He does. The Bible tells us, "Oh, the depth of the riches, both of the wisdom and knowledge of God! How unsearchable are His judgments and unfathomable His ways! For who has known the mind of the Lord, or who became His counselor?" (Romans 11:33–34). We can't figure God out. And you know what? I don't want to serve a God I can figure out. If we could, we'd hang right on His level and we wouldn't need Him at all. God knows the plot twists and turns that are coming, as well as the opportunities. Rest in this.

The key is to start where you are. What can you do, starting now, to begin living a mission-possible life?

Start Small

I love what Zechariah tells us: "Do not despise these small beginnings, for the LORD rejoices to see the work begin" (4:10, NLT).

You know where a mission-possible life begins? With an idea. With one thought, a single seed that contains potential. It just needs to be planted. An idea might come when you're faced with a need that's not being met. You might even get an idea when you meet someone. The Tim Tebow Foundation exists and is changing lives all over the world because of Sherwin. Sherwin is a boy with special needs whom I had met on a mission trip to the Philippines when I was a teenager. That one encounter planted an idea in my head and a hope in my heart that are still growing and expanding to this day.

Your idea may seem as small as helping someone with something he or she can't do. Don't brush it off. Even what's hidden to the naked eye, like the atom, has more power than we can imagine. It can change the world or even save a life.

If you're taking a walk or hanging with your friends outside and see a butterfly gliding through the air, what do you do? If you're like most people, you gasp in awe. You stop whatever you're doing and watch this winged creature float by with its coat of beautiful colors. You probably whip out your phone to snap a pic of its wonder. Butterflies are graceful and majestic. They have the power to stop people in their tracks with their gorgeousness.

But butterflies have a mortal enemy: rain. An average monarch butterfly, at five hundred milligrams, weighs about seven times as much as a large raindrop, a mass of roughly seventy milligrams.[1] One drop of water on a butterfly is like a person being pummeled by two water balloons the size of bowling bowls. You can imagine the damage a raindrop can do to the paper-thin wings of a butterfly. Most butterflies will sit out a rainstorm, for obvious reasons. But they have an armor within their wings to keep them from being destroyed.[2] When a raindrop hits the surface of a butterfly's wing, it ripples and spreads across the surface. A nanoscale wax layer repels the water while micro-bumps act like needles and pop each smaller drop. This powerful combination reduces the length of time and force of the contact the droplet has with the wing's surface, which consequently lowers the effect it has on the butterfly.

Butterflies have more to offer than just their captivating beauty. These tiny creatures contain optimized designs that can help solve challenges in the human world. Copying designs in nature for human purposes is known as biomimicry. Previous water-repellent products such as Gore-Tex, raincoats, and waterproof paint were created based on the design of the lotus leaf. Findings from the latest study on butterflies' wings could lead to more innovation.

There is more to the butterfly than meets the eye, and the same is true with the seeds God plants in our hearts. Be curious about the idea that appears before you. Look into it. Believe that God can use something small to do something great.

You might not realize the potential you have to live mission forward. You may not recognize the possibility that God can use you—yes, you!—to make a positive difference in the life of one or many. Here are some things you can do, starting now, to begin this journey:

- Research your options.
- Ask your parents for advice.
- Talk to people who have done similar things.
- Make a to-do list.
- Read books and listen to podcasts.
- Pray about it.
- Write down things you feel God may be speaking to you about.

Start small. Don't obsess about changing the world. Start by changing one person. Maybe that's yourself. Use what moves you, what God has put inside your heart, and take one step forward in mission-possible living.

When I Knew This Was It

When the team and I began talking about Night to Shine in 2014, we worked tirelessly for the next four or five months to build a game plan for something that we had never done before. There were so many moving parts: *How do we brand this the right way? What kind of rules do we need to set in place for our guests and our volunteers? What should the red carpet look like?* One of the biggest and most challenging questions we had was what to name the event.

Some options were Evening of Joy, A Night to Remember, Shine Bright, and Night of Hope. Although they weren't the worst ideas, I thought we could do better at creating a name that matched the brightness of the lives we would be celebrating. I could visualize Sherwin. I pictured him leaning on his escort while walking down a red carpet, literally shining—with joy and from camera flashes as volunteers photographed him and his fellow guests. I wanted these precious people to know their worth, and I wanted the world to see it as well.

I wanted our guests to experience a fun night in which they would be able to sense the glory of God shine on them. We finally landed on Night to Shine. The name encapsulated everything the evening was about. And in the next few months, we brainstormed, asking and researching and answering heaps of questions that we compiled in a twenty-one-page book summarizing the what, the why, and the how of Night to Shine. We have added to it every year, and it's now more than seventy-five pages.

I'll never forget the moment I knew for sure this event was what we were supposed to do. It was the Friday night before Valentine's Day 2015. We had partnered with forty-three churches in twenty-six states and three countries around the world to provide an unforgettable prom-night experience centered on God's love. I wish I were able to attend every event we host, but sadly I can't clone myself. I do spend the week leading up to Night to Shine visiting churches all over the world to pray with teams, encourage churches, and show love to would-be guests and volunteers. I also show up to as many undisclosed locations as I can the night of the event. I don't sleep much during that week, and it's the best kind of tired I know.

The first church on our itinerary in 2015 was the First Christian Church in North Carolina. All the planning, decision making, last-minute arrangements, and changing and making more changes led up to this moment. Butterflies exploded in my stomach. I felt the same nervousness and excitement I've felt right before playing in a national championship.

Rather than pulling up to the front of the church, I went to the side parking lot to keep the spotlight on all the wonderful guests of honor. I got out of the car and watched the beginning of the evening unfold. A long red carpet led from the curb to the front door of the church. On the sidelines, enthusiastic volunteers stood shoulder to shoulder, cheering for each guest as cameras flashed. I watched the first guest take his place, his arm draped around his escort. Decked out in a tux that looked too big for him, he flashed a smile and strutted down the red carpet with a confident swagger. I took a few steps closer and watched the next guest do the same. She was shier than the first. I could tell she wasn't sure how to process the lavish attention. Her hands trembled as she grabbed hold of her escort, eyes wide at the people cheering for her. Walking with careful steps, she made it to the end of the red carpet, face aglow with pride.

I went a bit closer, my eyes fixed on the long line of guests waiting for their turn to enter the prom, and then continued forward. My heart was overcome in that moment. This was it. This was part of my mission. This was the love of God in action. This was what it looks like to be embraced, accepted, and loved in the presence of His glory. It was hard to hold back the tears. I don't know how to best describe this in words, but as I crept closer to the crowd gathered at the beginning of the red carpet, it felt like I was swept up in a force field of God's protection. It felt like God was showing that He'd created each guest for a purpose and that they were loved without measure. Even though I'd had so many questions, His hand had guided the mission all along.

As I got closer to the crowd surrounding the red carpet, I said hello to a few people, shook some hands, and cheered for more guests. Then I noticed a girl about to make her way down the red carpet. I asked if I could walk her down. She said yes. Being able to escort her reminded me of the love and joy God brings to every one of His kings and queens all over the world.

When I got into the car late that night to go back home, I couldn't stop crying. It wasn't because it was a fun night or a cool prom; it was because the world came together to celebrate part of God's creation that isn't celebrated, loved, or walked down a red carpet as often or as much as it should be. The incredible feeling I had was better than the way I felt after even some of my biggest victories on the field. And the event wasn't even my idea. It was just my dream to take it around the world.

We did something good that night, and I wanted to do more of it.

I'm so glad we didn't turn back before we had all the answers. We would've missed out on so much goodness and joy and hope.

You don't know what God has in store for you when you step out and walk by faith. One idea or one thought that propels you into action, like dropping off a Bible to someone in need or welcoming people who don't feel as though they belong, can change the course of a person's day and even his or her life.

I'd like to share with you a letter that was written to our foundation from Jeneil, a volunteer at Night to Shine. It's one of my favorite letters we've ever received. Jeneil has a daughter, Rhema, who at the time of this writing is fourteen. At age two, Rhema was diagnosed with autism, apraxia (an incurable condition in which the brain is unable to make and deliver instructions to the body), and a rare and stubborn seizure disorder. Because of these conditions, she is unable to speak. A doctor once told Jeneil that Rhema would most likely never comprehend language, a condition also known as word deafness. "I thought it was all a cruel cosmic joke," Jeneil said. "My child's name means 'word,' yet she could not speak or understand a word."

When the opportunity to volunteer for Night to Shine arose, Jeneil couldn't wait to sign up. Here's what she had to say:

So it goes, in God's economy, the ones who intend to help/volunteer/bless others are the ones who get doubly blessed in return.

I once said that when you have a child with special needs, every child with special needs is your child. So perhaps you can imagine my joy, multiplied by one hundred, seeing our guests lavishly loved and treasured and honored with a night that was made just for them.

There have been times I've wanted to shout to everyone and no one in particular, "Don't forget my girl. It's not easy, I know. But she's here, sitting in the dark, waiting for you to sit with her, see her, know her. Don't forget my girl."

At Night to Shine, God whispered to me, "I will never ever forget her. She is famous to Me like an A-lister walking the red carpet. I throw a party, serve the best food, and clothe her in love. I pamper her with my goodness and put a crown on her head. She is precious, and she is Mine."

How extravagant is the love of God for us.

God loves us. He does not forget us. There is no one who sits alone in the dark whom He doesn't see.

You might feel as though you're alone in the dark as you begin to figure out what it means to live mission possible. That's okay. Remember, you don't have to be perfect or know it all or be known or seen by everyone. You just have to trust the One who does know and see you. Take heart: God's in it with you.

If you feel uncertain as to where to start, I want to remind you to start small. What does the Bible ask you to do? While some of the Bible is hard to understand, our calling as believers is pretty simple. I, for one, am so glad He made that practical. Help the needy? Love? Defend the defenseless? Be merciful and kind? Yes to all those things.

In the Great Commission, Jesus told His followers to go and make disciples of all nations. You don't have to be a pastor, a Sunday school teacher, or a missionary to do this. Do it as you go. Do it as you get your homework and chores done. Do it as you prepare for your game. Do it as you eat lunch with your friends in the cafeteria or welcome a new student at school. Be the light Jesus has been to you wherever you may be.

We are called to love God and to love people. The best definition of the verb form of *love* that I know is to choose the best interests of another person over your own and act on his or her behalf. Let's find people who need love and act on their behalf.

When you are willing to be used by God, He will open your eyes to opportunities to step in and fill a gap. It's okay to feel afraid or have questions while taking the first step. Do it anyway. Living mission possible starts with one step. What are you willing to do?

6

Purpose in the Resistance

There is no success without hardship.
—SOPHOCLES

Weighing barely four pounds, Manuel Alfredo, nicknamed Alfredito, was born two months early in October 2003. His parents, Irene and Alfredo Salazar, and their two daughters couldn't wait to take him home when he was finally discharged after a one-month stay in the neonatal ICU. Alfredito brought much joy to his family. Although his growth and neurological development were slightly below average because he was premature, he was a happy and sweet baby.

When Alfredito was eight months old, his parents took him to the pediatrician, who made a shocking discovery: Their baby had Down syndrome. The Salazars left the doctor's office that day in tears. They thought, *How could we have missed this? What does this mean for Alfredito? How will our lives change? What are we going to do?*

The response they received from some friends and family was even worse than their own questions. One woman immediately burst into tears and said, "Why did God do this to you? You serve Him." Her sadness made them feel as though Alfredito were a mistake. Many people reacted to the baby's diagnosis quietly or apologetically. Thankfully, there were others who were more encouraging.

When Alfredito was a year old, more bad news: Doctors discovered five defects in his heart that demanded open-heart surgery. The operation was rescheduled multiple times for a variety of reasons. It looked as if Alfredito would never get the surgery. But then a miracle happened: The surgery was finally scheduled, and the little boy recovered brilliantly.

During this frustrating period, Alfredito's parents were beginning to see the world of special needs for the first time. They discovered that many families where they lived did not have access to adequate care for Down syndrome, and they wanted to help. In 2005, the Salazars founded Down Guatemala, an organization that provides support, education, and therapy to children with Down syndrome in Guatemala City. At the time, there were almost no organizations like it in their country. The couple didn't have much money, so to fund the ministry, they sold their home. They didn't receive a ton of donations at first, so they continued to donate their own money and sell whatever possessions they had, including their cars. They spent all of their savings to keep the organization alive.

If you want to live a life that counts, be prepared to sacrifice. The Salazars were willing to give up their material possessions, even necessities like a car, for a mission they believed in. It got uncomfortable for them. But that's what happens when we sacrifice. It may not feel good at the time, but it is doing greater work within us. And it is giving us a chance to see what is possible only through God.

In October 2020, Down Guatemala celebrated its fifteenth anniversary. The organization has served more than 350 families, of which 65 percent are Indigenous (of Mayan descent) and do not have access to resources about the condition. Irene Salazar told me, "We have realized that everything we have on this earth does not belong to us. We are only administrators of it, and if the owner, who is God, asks you to give it, you must give it with joy. He is the owner, and He knows what is best for our lives and our ministries."

Sacrifice is not the most pleasing word. It might bring to mind the need to give it all up or to give until it hurts. While making sacrifices may not feel as good as a nap on a cold rainy day, it has its benefits. One study published in *Social Psychological and Personality Science* reported that we find greater happiness when we deny ourselves, even temporarily, something pleasurable, like chocolate bars.[1] When we live mission possible, sacrifice is inevitable. But rather than looking at sacrifice as something negative, we should see it as something to embrace.

I doubt that the Salazars were outright excited about having to sell their car or the home they loved, but I know that when they were able to help the first family who walked through the doors of Down Guatemala, it was all worth it.

They know the true meaning of sacrifice: giving up what you want *now* for what you want *most*.

Go Ahead, Get Uncomfortable

One of the greatest obstacles to living a mission-possible life is the pursuit of comfort. French scientist Alexis de Tocqueville came to the United States in 1831 to write a big book called *Democracy in America*. After conducting more than two hundred interviews and visiting seventeen states in nine months, he wrote over eight hundred pages on what he saw as the most democratic and flourishing nation on earth. In an essay titled "On the Taste for Material Well-Being in America," de Tocqueville noted that those living in the United States "are universally preoccupied with meeting the body's every need and attending to life's little comforts."[2] It wasn't a compliment. He was saying that Americans were concerned with being as comfortable as possible.

Yikes!

Remember, the Frenchman wrote this in 1831. This was before smartphones and social media and smart cars and Google and washing machines and drive-throughs and Postmates and overnight shipping and virtual education. But even then, Americans were focused on making themselves as comfortable as possible. Wow. Could you imagine what de Tocqueville would have to say today? I'm sort of embarrassed that his truth bomb explodes with even more power almost two centuries later!

Comfort is, well, comfortable. It's warm and cozy and loves to tempt us to stay longer than we promised ourselves we would. But when we choose to sacrifice mission-possible lives for the path of least resistance, we actually suffer. We stop growing. Sure, we may experience less stress, but we also miss out on untapped adventures. Sometimes you just have to be the first one to get uncomfortable, especially when everyone is watching.

For parts of my life, one of the things I was most passionate about and willing to sacrifice for was sports. I'd be the first one up and the last one to go to sleep. I'd wake up at midnight sometimes just to train because I knew no one else was doing it. I didn't mind making myself uncomfortable on purpose if it meant I would gain greater physical ability or the respect of my teammates. I love what financial guru Dave Ramsey has said: "If you will live like no one else, later you can live like no one else."[3] Sometimes you just have to make a statement in order to do this.

During the early weeks of my freshman year at the University of Florida, our coaches and trainers led us in one of our first major workouts, called the Harley-Davidson. I think one of their goals was to train our brains into never giving in and never giving up. One day, my teammates and I worked our muscles into overtime with sled pushes until our legs couldn't move another inch, wall squats until our muscles quivered into useless piles of Jell-O, and tug-of-war battles in which the rope ended up coated in the blood from our hands. I'm pretty sure most of us were puking by the time we were done.

As if that weren't enough, while we were still wiping the vomit off our lips, our trainers had more marching orders on their agenda.

"Get in the cold tub and start recovering. All of you. Up to your hips. Just seven minutes. Let's go!" Ice baths, a form of cryotherapy, are great for athletes. They decrease soreness, reduce swelling and muscle damage, and speed recovery so you can push it harder the next workout or game or race. They're also completely not fun. No one wants to do them, including me.

My teammates and I gathered around the tubs in the room. I stood by as they looked at the freezing water. They pointed at the tubs. They started talking and complaining about them. They did just about everything but actually get in the tubs.

"Let's go!" a voice from the training room yelled. "Gotta get in for seven minutes. Move!"

My teammates, some of the biggest and baddest ballers I knew, were freaking out. There was more talking, but no one moved. After more yelling from the training room, a few of the guys stepped into the tub and got in maybe to their knees, yapping and yelling the farther they dipped themselves into the ice-cold water.

"Get your hips in, guys. Let's go!"

Watching everyone complain and joke and continue to resist what they were going to have to do anyway, I quietly stepped aside from the crowd and took a few steps forward to the cold tub. Without saying a word, I crept inside. My toes immediately contracted. Sinking deeper as I squatted into the tub, my skin burned and my muscles stung. Although I needed to plunge my body only up to my hips, I dipped farther into the frigid tub until just my head bobbed out of the water. On the inside, I was dying, my skin frozen in shock. To everyone on the outside, my poker face was on point. It was a walk in the park. *Yawn.*

This was a mission. See, I didn't want to just get the guys to like me; I needed them to respect me. In sports, respect is more important than being liked. I wanted to be a great quarterback and a great leader. I knew that if my teammates respected me, they would play hard for me. Sure, part of this had to do with ego. I needed the guys to think of me as a different kind of animal who looked at pain differently. But this was also an opportunity to set the tone of who I was and what I was about. I was telling them without words that I was willing to go to the nth degree to get uncomfortable for something greater.

Making a big deal out of getting in a cold tub may seem silly to you, but I gained cred that day. If my teammates respected me that much for being the first to get uncomfortable and going the extra mile, then they would do the same for me one day. I wanted to have an impact on my team. I didn't want to get into an ice-cold tub up to my neck. But I would gladly do it again if my teammates would think, *That guy is doing anything he can, so I might go a little bit further to do what I can too.*

Oh, yeah, it was definitely cold. But here's a tip: If you get through the first two and a half minutes, the rest is easy. That's true of almost every good hard thing, isn't it? The toughest part is almost always the start.

I believe that every single one of us has that choice. We can do hard, uncomfortable things that stretch us and don't feel good, because we know there are greater gains. When's the last time you had an opportunity to show others who you really are by getting uncomfortable?

Is It a Setback or a Setup?

In 1 Corinthians 16:8–9, there's a telling statement from Paul: "I will stay in Ephesus until Pentecost, for a wide door for effective work has opened to me, and there are many adversaries" (ESV). *The Message* puts it like this: "A huge door of opportunity for good work has opened up here. (There is also mushrooming opposition.)"

Paul was writing this from the city of Ephesus. He had planned to stay there for just a little while but ended up staying longer. During his stay, many people came to know Jesus, and Paul performed many miracles. But because of Paul's success, dangerous enemies popped up and tried to ruin the good he was doing. Not everyone was Paul's biggest fan. At the time of writing 1 Corinthians, he had no idea that this "mushrooming opposition" would result in a riot in Ephesus, causing him to leave for Macedonia (see Acts 19:23–20:1). In other passages, he described his opposition as fighting with wild beasts and as an excessive burden (see 1 Corinthians 15:32; 2 Corinthians 1:8). Paul didn't let the resistance keep him from his mission, however. In fact, he doubled down. He shared the gospel with even more passion. He used the "mushrooming opposition" to push himself forward.

Human beings were created with a fight-or-flight response. This is an inner physiological reaction that happens when we feel threatened. In simple terms, we're wired to handle stress. Biologically speaking, our body's stress response was designed to help us survive. Researchers at Berkeley have found that some stress can actually be good for us. Daniela Kaufer, associate professor of integrative biology, has discovered that short-lived stress actually "primes the brain for improved performance."[4] This is referred to as stress-related growth, or physiological thriving.

Kaufer is not alone in her findings. Research indicates that stress can affect our well-being in a positive way if we have the right perspective.

When our foundation hires employees, one of the essentials we look for is whether they have had to deal with strong resistance or hardship in the past. We want to understand if and how they endured something tough. Did they stay the course? Did they remain faithful? Did the opposition make them better, create more wisdom in them, or prepare them for the next battle? We want to partner with people who have faced strong resistance and grown through that experience.

What challenges are you facing today as you strive to live mission possible? Do you feel as though you're too young to do anything important? Do the people who are supposed to love you the most make you feel less than? Are you worried that you'll never get past certain mistakes or that you're not good enough to even try to live mission possible? Hang in there! Don't give up.

You don't know the doors that are just about to open for you.

When you flip your perspective on the uncomfortable, you may find that a setback can look a lot more like a setup. Think about it this way: If Daniel's journey hadn't included his being kidnapped, taken into a new culture, and having his character attacked, I doubt he would have been prepared to shine when he faced the lions. The same can be said about Joseph in the book of Genesis. If Joseph hadn't been betrayed by his own brothers and later by his coworkers, who knows if he would have had a chance to become the second most powerful man in Egypt and be able to help his starving family. If the stakes hadn't been so high for Queen Esther, she wouldn't have been in a position to save an entire nation of people.

None of those individuals had an easy go in life. They suffered. They were betrayed. They were persecuted. I imagine in those pressing times of hardship, they probably even questioned God's plan for their lives.

But allow me to remind you of what Paul wrote: "I can do all things through Him who strengthens me" (Philippians 4:13). When we embrace the resistance, we get stronger. We build up stamina to continue to run the race. When we exercise our muscles, they get microtears. When we keep exercising consistently, the microtears build up to form muscle mass. In a sense, our bodies have to be broken down to come back stronger. The same can be true of our lives. What you think of as a setback just might be a setup that takes you where God wants you to go.

Remember the Big Picture: Eternity

Paul didn't allow the resistance he faced—from people who hated and wanted to destroy him to being thrown into prison multiple times—to cause him to give up. He knew a little secret: "Our momentary, light affliction is producing for us an eternal weight of glory far beyond all comparison, while we look not at the things which are seen, but at the things which are not seen; for the things which are seen are temporal, but the things which are not seen are eternal" (2 Corinthians 4:17–18). Paul understood that there is more to life than what we see.

When you live mission possible, you invest in eternity. You may not get to play a lot of video games, but your fulfillment will be earth shattering. Live today and each day forward with a forever mindset. Focus on doing things that will matter even years from now.

Remember Daddy's Dollars? After a few years of doing my best to get the most dollars by doing things like helping my neighbor with his chicken farm, by the time I was around ten years old, I had a lot of money saved. (At least from the perspective of a little kid.)

By watching some of my siblings, I learned quickly to save the cash and not spend it. I'd seen too often one of them rush out to buy a video game or a cool shirt and then have little to no money left over. I had also watched my dad work tirelessly to help the people he served in the Philippines. I learned early on what a lucky little boy I was. Unlike some of the children served by Dad and his team, I always had something to eat. I had a roof over my head. I had shoes on my feet. I had a mom and a dad. It broke my heart to see children who didn't have those things. I wanted to do something about it, but I was just a kid. I didn't have much, but I wanted to use what I had—at the time, my accumulation of Daddy's Dollars—to make a difference. I was determined to use the money I had saved for good.

The Bible tells us that faith, hope, and love will last for all time and that the greatest of these is love. Is there any better way to show Jesus to others than to give to them, serve them, or help them? Doing so is a form of love, and it is something that will have an eternal impact.

As a boy, I dreamed of one day making a million dollars and giving it away. But at the time, all I had were the Daddy's Dollars I had earned, and I always gave my dad some of *that* money to bring with him to the Philippines. I wanted to help kids who didn't have much. Dad would always come back from his trips and tell me story after story about how even my chump change was enough to buy a little boy or girl my age a pair of flip-flops, a bag of food for the child's family, or even a Bible. Even though it may have been more fun to buy a video game with that money, I was beginning to understand what it meant to live a mission-possible life. It's about making a difference, loving the least of these, and fighting for those who can't fight for themselves. And I wanted to do more of it.

At the time of this writing, Alfredito is seventeen years old. He is a swim star and has even won a bronze medal in the Latin American games of the Special Olympics. Alfredito's diagnosis may have changed the plans his parents had for their future, but it's been a change for the better! And it has also changed the lives of hundreds of other kids and their families who have had the opportunity to lock arms with Down Guatemala.

Don't run from the resistance.

Remember, there is always a purpose to the pain.

7

Elevate Convictions over Emotions

Though our feelings come and go,
[God's] love for us does not.
—C. S. Lewis

W hen you stand in front of a $1.5 billion mixed-use mega complex glistening in the Texas sun, you can't help but feel that you are standing in the presence of greatness. The Star's ninety-one acres hold the no-expense-spared corporate head-quarters and entertainment complex of the Dallas Cowboys. Anchored by the luxury Omni Hotel and the Ford Center, this state-of-the-art twelve-thousand-seat indoor arena houses the NFL team as well as eight high school teams; it's a breathtaking beauty.

I touched down in Texas that morning because I was sched-uled to speak later at the Omni. At the time, I didn't even realize that the hotel was part of the Cowboys' complex. It was a cool coincidence. And it was fun to tour the facilities before the event.

Every turn down every hallway and into every room made my jaw drop even farther. I mean, have you ever seen a football-shaped locker room? Or a hot tub the size of your neighbor's swimming pool? The exercise facility that was open to guests (guests!) was even better than some of the NFL weight rooms I'd been in over the years.

I was psyched to be able to encourage a couple hundred people later that night at a speaking event, but as I walked around the complex, I felt myself getting bummed out. Where I *was* reminded me of where I *wasn't*.

The Reality of Our Feelings

As I walked around the Star, I became swept up in unmet longings. Dreams unfulfilled. Questions that I may never have answers to. Thoughts swirled in my head:

- *I wish I had a chance to be a player in this facility.*
- *I wish I had what they have.*
- *I wish I would have . . .*
- *I wish I did . . .*

Then came the finger pointing.

- *God, I wish You had a different plan.*

Seeing the Cowboys' facilities made me miss football. It reminded me of what I didn't have—or, rather, what I wasn't playing. I found myself wrapped up in this strange mix of depression, selfishness, bitterness, and envy. I hated it. I try to be a pretty good gatekeeper of negative feelings, but those crashed the party.

I found myself inwardly in a funk right until the moment I walked onstage at the event hours later. I was able to share with a group of amazing people, but my joy was diminished up until that moment because I had fixed my focus on what I *didn't* have. That's not how I wanted that day to go. My mission that day was to have an impact on a bunch of souls and give hope to those who needed it. Instead, I was totally caught off guard by an emotional sucker punch.

Have you ever had a similar experience? Have you watched someone else get the spot on the team or the role in the play you worked so hard for? Or gotten frustrated because your sister hardly studies and aces her tests while you hit the books all the time and barely churn out Bs? Feelings can get the best of us, can't they?

Feelings aren't all negative or even just a necessary evil. God created us with feelings. I love what Helen Keller said: "The best and most beautiful things in the world cannot be seen or even touched. They must be felt with the heart."[1]

We were born to feel. And it's okay to have feelings. I think about my mom: from having the courage to be one of the first parents to homeschool their children, to packing up her family and moving to a mission field in the Philippines, to almost dying because of her high-risk pregnancy with me, to the countless occasions on which she and Dad had no money and no food on the table but believed God would provide. At times, she must have felt overwhelmed, tired, afraid, and stressed out. Though she didn't wallow in those feelings, she definitely had them. She chose to pray about them and give them to God, which she did often!

While emotions are a sign of what we're going through, they don't have to be the boss of us.

Choose the Right Wolf

When negative feelings overwhelm us, we tend to stay in that dark place for much longer than we should. Looking back on that afternoon walking around the Cowboys' headquarters, I probably didn't need to stay bummed out as long as I did. I'm not saying I should have immediately snapped out of my funk. I'm not a robot. None of us are.

While emotions aren't something we can always control, we need to figure out what to do when they hit us so we don't get stuck. There's an old legend about two wolves that is sometimes attributed to the Cherokee Nation. An old Indian chief is teaching his grandson lessons about life. "There is a fight going on inside me between two wolves. One is evil, full of hatred, greed, anger, jealousy, lies, and selfishness, and the other is good, full of kindness, love, grace, mercy, and humility. The same fight is going on inside of you." The grandson thinks for a minute, then asks the chief, "Which wolf will win?"

"The one you feed," replies his grandfather.

In the stadium that day, I didn't have to allow envy and bitterness to hang out for such a long time. I could have starved those feelings by focusing on what I did have in the moment: an absolutely amazing opportunity to bless a group of incredible men and women and show appreciation for who they are and what they do. I could have fed those thoughts with my attention.

We have a choice. We always do. We can soak in our misery, or we can turn over those negative emotions to God. Jesus gives us a way out of our funk. Take a look at what the Bible says:

> Come to Me, all who are weary and burdened, and I will give you rest. Take My yoke upon you and learn from Me, for I am gentle and humble in heart, and you will find rest for your souls. (Matthew 11:28–29)

On the evening of January 8, 2009, the Florida Gators would face the Oklahoma Sooners in Miami for the national championship game. I remember sitting in my hotel room that afternoon during the three-hour break Coach Urban gave us. I was super nervous, so I decided to hold an impromptu Bible study. My teammates and also Pastor Lindsey Seals, our chaplain, started filling up the room, one by one, until we reached capacity. There was so much tension in the room from the pressure. In reading the above passage from Matthew, I began to try to encourage the guys: "Our weight feels heavy right now, but we have the choice to give it to God, for He is gentle and humble in heart." Pastor Lindsey brought a guitar and started leading us in worship songs. We each left the room a little bit lighter and a little bit brighter. That's what happens when we give God what we cannot carry any longer.

Jesus invites, welcomes, and encourages everyone—the weak, the miserable, the overwhelmed, the hopeless, the tired—to "come" to Him. And He says, "I will give you rest" (verse 28).

Psalm 55:22 is another reminder to give our problems to Him: "Cast your burden upon the LORD and He will sustain you." *The Message* Bible paraphrases it, "Pile your troubles on GOD's shoulders—he'll carry your load, he'll help you out."

The Bible doesn't teach us that we will never have burdens. In fact, Jesus says we will! "These things I have spoken to you so that in Me you may have peace. In the world you have tribulation, but take courage; I have overcome the world" (John 16:33). Notice what He says after He tells us life isn't going to be easy: "Take courage." We can hope. We can choose courage and trust in Jesus, even if our feelings don't match up in the moment. And instead of allowing feelings to overtake us, we can focus on what we are called to do: live mission possible.

Instead of isolating ourselves, we can love God.

Instead of feeling bitter, we can love people.

Instead of being selfish, we can put the interests of others above our own.

Instead of complaining, we can serve.

Instead of being paralyzed by fear, we can take action.

When we begin to realize the unshakable character of God, whatever comes our way, we can stand firm and live by our convictions.

The Power of Conviction

Conviction is a firm belief. I like how David Jeremiah defined it: "a fixed belief, a deeply held set of certainties that lodges in the center of your mind and heart."[2]

Convictions aren't merely opinions. They don't change based on your mood or what position you get on the team. When you are faced with a choice, your convictions will cause you to do the right thing rather than react to what your feelings are telling you.

I believe I'm here on this earth for a reason—that God has a purpose and a plan for my life. In fact, that's a conviction I live by. I believe it even when I'm tired or struggling with making the right decisions. And I believe it's true for you too.

I have learned that convictions are stronger than emotions. Emotions will lie to you. Emotions will tell you when your alarm goes off in the morning that you're too tired, that you didn't get enough sleep, that you deserve to snooze, that you'll get up early tomorrow (for real this time). But if you listen to your convictions instead of your emotions, you'll be the first one up. You'll be the last one standing. You'll run through the pain. You'll keep building the boat even when the sky is clear. You'll do things you may not necessarily want to because it puts the interests of others before your own.

Demi and I share many common interests: our faith, for one. We also love spending time with family and are both health conscious. But we also have our differences. For starters, she loves dressing up and going out to dinner. I, on the other hand, couldn't care less about going out on the town. I'm on the road often, so when I have free time, I want to enjoy food in the comfort and privacy of my own home. But my feelings are not my only priority. The second I said "I do," I signed up for more than my emotions. I live by the conviction that I love Demi and that instead of doing whatever I want all the time, I serve her in ways that matter to her. I take a drive even when I'm tired. I go to a restaurant even when I feel like staying in. I walk along a beach even though I hate sand. I do all these things for Demi, and though I wouldn't usually get joy from the activities themselves, I am happy, truly, because my wife is happy. That brings me joy.

Although I know that I make mistakes, I still strive to live by my convictions. I try my best to love Demi in a sacrificial way and grow better each day at being the husband she deserves. Feelings fade and change like seasons, but when you base your actions, your attitude, your decisions, and your behavior on your convictions, most of the time you can expect a positive outcome. But there's one conviction that will never disappoint us, even when life doesn't turn out the way we planned or expected.

Holy Confidence

As Christians, our convictions must rest in our identity in God and in who He is. The Bible tells us that "Jesus Christ is the same yesterday and today, and forever" (Hebrews 13:8). In every season and circumstance, we can trust the character of God! Scripture gives us a thorough picture of His very nature.

God is holy, righteous, just, merciful, loving, kind, faithful, gracious, compassionate, good, and wise, to name several attributes.[3] God loved us so much that He severed a perfect relationship with His Son so we could be made right with Him. He gave up His child for you and for me. I don't know about you, but that's someone I can trust.

We may wrestle with not knowing or liking the plans God has

for us. Maybe you wish you had different talents and abilities or that you lived somewhere else or that your classes weren't so hard. Maybe you're frustrated because you see only one of your parents on the weekend or you're constantly changing schools. In those times, choose to cast your cares on Jesus and trust in the character of God. We may not know or understand what God is doing or where He is taking us, but we can take to heart His words:

My thoughts are not your thoughts,
Nor are your ways My ways. . . .
For as the heavens are higher than the earth,
So are My ways higher than your ways
And My thoughts than your thoughts. (Isaiah 55:8–9)

God has given us His best—His Son—and has proved that He can be trusted. I may not understand why certain roads have started or ended, but I can count on His faithfulness. I know that sounds so simple—and it's powerful if lived out—but there are times I fail to remember this truth. It's mind boggling to me. I've been a Christian most of my life, almost thirty years, yet I still allow myself to worry about the stupidest things or let my emotions rob me of the best of my days. Cue the scene of me walking around the Cowboys' complex sulking because I'm not playing football. I forget that I can trust God because He gave up His best, His only Son, for me. When I remind myself of that truth, my funk begins to disappear.

The Bible tells us that one day Jesus got heartbreaking news. I'll preface this story by saying that John the Baptist was Jesus's cousin. He also played a major role in His life: John announced his cousin's arrival to the people of Israel, and he also had the privilege of baptizing Him. But something terrible had happened to John. He was thrown into jail by King Herod and later killed.

When John's disciples shared the horrible news with Jesus, He was crushed. His cousin, his friend, his partner in sharing that "the kingdom of heaven is at hand" was dead. When Jesus found out, He did what most of us would do in this situation: He went off somewhere by Himself. He tried to withdraw to a desolate place to be alone. He turned His phone off. He ignored the knocks at the door. Of course He did. Jesus wanted to grieve, by Himself, for someone He loved so much. But He didn't get to do this right away.

While Jesus was attempting to go to a private location by boat, the crowds found out where He was and, of course, wanted to follow Him. When Jesus got out of the boat, a throng of people was waiting for Him, wanting Him to teach them and pray with them and perform miracles for them. What do you think Jesus's response was? Do you think He was peeved? Do you think He muttered something unmentionable under His breath? Do you think He threw His hands up toward heaven and yelled, "Can't I have one minute alone, please?" No, the Bible tells us that He "felt compassion for them and healed their sick" (Matthew 14:14). Instead of being by Himself when His heart was hurting so bad, He taught the people. He interacted with them. He healed the sick. And in one of the greatest miracles in the Bible, Jesus fed this crowd of more than five thousand people with only five loaves of bread and two fish, a lunch given to Him by a little boy (see verses 15–21). I can't imagine Jesus was in the perfect frame of mind to perform miracles that afternoon, yet He lived by His convictions. What an example for us.

Emotions will never be the same all the time. They're up one day and down the next. They may be good, like joy or gratitude, but they might also take a darker route, like pride or jealousy. But convictions offer consistency. When your convictions are rooted in who you are and in living a mission-possible life, they will drive you to do the right thing. When feelings tell you to call it quits, your convictions will remind you that you can push a little harder or go a little further to reach your goal. When your emotions tell you that "good enough" is good enough, your convictions make you realize that you can be better.

Life isn't always easy, and we won't always get what we want, but we get to trust that God loves us because He demonstrated it. We didn't love Him first. He loved us first. And when we live by that conviction, we can rest with a holy confidence that "all things . . . work together for good to those who love God, to those who are called according to His purpose" (Romans 8:28).

8

Embrace the Grind

It is no use saying, "We are doing our best." You have got to succeed in doing what is necessary.
—Winston Churchill

If there's a paradise on earth, it would have to be the Maldives, where Demi and I honeymooned at the beginning of 2020. Made up of more than a thousand islands, some of which are uninhabitable and nothing more than isolated strips of sand, this country looks like the stock photos you see of crystalline beaches and whimsical overwater villas atop turquoise seas that beg you to take a dip. The place where we stayed sat in the middle of the Indian Ocean. Nothing but miles and miles of fifty breathtaking shades of blue under clear skies.

While I like to think of myself as an action guy—I am, after all, the one who arranges snake-wrangling competitions and kayak races on the Tebow family vacations—this was definitely more of a laid-back atmosphere. Lots of snorkeling, swimming, and sunbathing. There were maybe forty or fifty people on the whole island, so it often felt like we were the only ones there.

I think it was on the fifth day that we enjoyed our first-ever stargazing dinner. Our resort offered an observatory that hosts one of the largest overwater telescopes in the Indian Ocean. A few tables surrounded this massive telescope, which was connected to a screen on each table. After we ordered our dinner, an astronomer who worked there showed us around the galaxies of the northern and southern hemispheres. As he navigated the skies, my wife and I took turns gaping in awe through the telescope.

When our dinner arrived, we traded the telescopic view of the skies for savoring each bite of our mouthwatering cuisine. I don't know what smelled better, the refreshing saltwater scent of the open ocean or the robust aroma of filet mignon. With the lagoon's gentle waves lapping around us and with no other plans for the evening besides enjoying this magical place, I was the most relaxed I'd ever been. Being completely at rest is really challenging for me. It doesn't come naturally. But as I tuned into Demi's sweet voice and soft music played in the background, it was easy to focus on this rare time of quiet together.

Suddenly a screech erupted from the main area of the resort about 150 feet away, making Demi and me both jump out of our seats. It was followed by an outburst of angry voices. Instinct took over and I practically hurdled the table—and Demi—as I took off at high speed to see what the commotion was about.

"Where are you going?" Demi called out.

"I have to go check what's wrong!" I yelled back as I raced down the snaking jetty over the lagoon. Trust me, before I took off, I made sure that Demi was not in any danger at all. I would never do anything to jeopardize my wife's safety, but I knew I had to do something!

As I got closer to the scene, I discovered the source of the ruckus. It was absolute chaos. Ten or so adults were screaming at each other in a language I didn't understand, their faces flushed with rage. Half-eaten meals were splattered all over the floor. Broken glass from stemware covered the now filthy table. I had no idea what anyone was saying or what they were fighting about. Some staff tried to help calm tempers, and more arrived on the scene just after I got there. They did a great job of cooling a heated atmosphere.

From what I could gather in speaking to a staff member later, the event was a dinner party made up of two families. What started out as a harmless argument turned ugly when one family took deep offense.

But this story isn't about a family fight. It's about making each day, each moment, count. It's about saying yes when it matters and being ready when opportunity strikes. It's about being prepared and willing to step up when the occasion arises.

I may not have won the Best Date award that evening when I bolted from our stargazing dinner to check out the problem and see if I could assist, but I would rather choose to help over doing nothing any day.

I may have been on my honeymoon, but that didn't mean the

mission-possible part of me was on vacation. I want it to be who I am. If there's a problem, I am going to see if I can help in any way.

Power in the Details

Not every day is game day. Not every day is a day that our foundation executes a raid to rescue people who are hurting or in need. Not every day is a day we grant a sick child a W15H. Not every day is a day we get to bring a special-needs orphan to his or her new forever family. But every day is a day we get to push the mission forward. This means that every day we are doing research, making phone calls, setting up appointments, having meetings, creating budgets, finding sponsors, and so much more. You know what a lot of this is? The grind. Putting in the hard, necessary, and daily work. It's not very glamorous; people on the outside don't see it and don't realize how hard it is or what it takes to get it done. The grind can be mundane. It's like practicing the same shot a million times or studying the same thing for hours.

Those moments don't have the payoff, but if you don't put in those moments, you'll never get the payoff. What's just as important as game day is the accumulative value of the practices and training put in on Tuesday morning and Wednesday night and Thursday afternoon. In fact, the tip-off matters more when each day that week you attacked your drills for hours when no one was watching. You have to make a random Tuesday just as important as national championship day. The English writer Alan Armstrong said, "Champions do not become champions when they win the event, but in the hours, weeks, months and years they spend preparing for it. The victorious performance itself is merely the demonstration of their championship character."[1] This is the mindset of hard work, practice, grit, endurance—all ingredients that dreams are made of.

You don't have to be an athlete to engage in life with this kind of intensity; you just have to live mission possible. There is nothing neutral about living a mission-possible life.

I think of our W15H program. Since we started this program in 2011, nearly one hundred children and teenagers with life-threatening illnesses have received an official all-inclusive experience sponsored by our foundation. This includes a weekend of customized activities, gifts, meals, and time with me. (Hundreds of Brighter Day experiences have also been provided, which include hospital visits, phone calls, and video chats.) So many weekends come to mind, but I especially remember the one with brothers Andrew, twelve at the time, and Aaron, thirteen. Both brothers were diagnosed with a rare form of brain tumor. Their weekend was a big moment for everyone involved since it was a double W15H. It took place in Atlanta at the 2019 SEC Championship Game, Georgia versus Louisiana State University. We had a great time teasing each other about our rival sports teams.

I also got to spend a weekend with Ben, a kind thirteen-year-old who has cystic fibrosis. Ben and I discussed how God uses our difficult seasons for His glory. We also talked about the importance of our daily routine of eating healthy and exercise and how that makes us better athletes. And I'll never forget the W15H weekend with Josh, a courageous young man from Mississippi who had brain cancer. It was an emotional night for all in the room, and it was so special to see God working in his life. Though the W15H eventually comes to a close, our relationships with these families do not. They will always be permanent members of the TTF family.

Putting together a W15H weekend is no easy task. The week of the W15H, Kelsey, who heads our program at TTF, resembles a blur as she darts in and out of the office, running up and down the stairs to prepare merch, and is constantly on the phone scheduling and rescheduling, and rescheduling the rescheduled schedules. Here's a peek into the process of a W15H so you get an idea of what I'm talking about.

A W15H request comes in and Kelsey connects with the family and the child. Without promising anything, she finds out what we can do to show their son or daughter our support. She also has to confirm via a doctor's note that the illness or disease is in fact life threatening. (Yes, we've had situations where that was not the case.) And from there, her checklist is about a mile long and includes working with the child and parents to fill out his or her favorite things (color, superhero, sport, movie, hobby, song, book, snack), budgeting the weekend, arranging flights and hotel accommodations, making restaurant reservations, decorating their weekend hotel room with all the child's favorite things, planning special activities, arranging gifts, coordinating arrival and departure for each event on the itinerary, and coordinating logistics with *SEC Nation* or whatever cool event we are part of that weekend. The responsibilities I mentioned are just a glimpse of the details that need to be ironed out to make a weekend perfect for a child and his or her family.

Before the pandemic, I didn't know where I would be on the weekend until the Sunday before, and then Kelsey would have four days to arrange all the details. I was traveling so often, especially during baseball season, that there were times I would spring a W15H weekend on her two days before. And although to the human eye that feat seemed close to impossible to accomplish in such a short amount of time, Kelsey would accept the mission with a smile—and get it done. I never saw her sweat, either, but I'm sure she probably did.

Because she had planned in advance (by regularly checking our merch inventory, staying in touch with families, and researching information even before she needed to), when I would tell her, for instance, that I was going to be in Charlotte that next weekend and was wondering if she could find a child there for us to celebrate, she was able to track one down on a moment's notice. Oh, it was still stressful for her, and many times she wondered how on earth she was going to pull it off, but by the grace of God, every W15H weekend exceeded my expectations.

Kelsey attends every W15H weekend to ensure everything runs smoothly. I'm glad she gets to witness the fruits of her labor. The look on the face of a child who walks into a hotel room that has been decked out in his or her favorite colors and superhero decor is priceless. Even more so is getting the opportunity to experience the faith, hope, and love these children, who battle life and death every day, share with us. Kelsey says, "We at the foundation often say that although most people think we are blessing the family, any one of us who are there know that we are the ones who walk away so encouraged." It's humbling to have a child who knows the true meaning of suffering and pain look into your eyes and tell you with confidence, "God is good, and I believe He can heal me."

There's power in the details.

There's purpose in being prepared.

When you pursue the grind with purpose and devote yourself wholly to living mission possible, even on your honeymoon or the day after the national championship, you continue to prepare yourself for the next moment that comes. And the next, and the one after that. What might that look like for you? Not waiting until the last minute to get an assignment done, planning ahead when you can, keeping track of your schedule so you don't get to the end of the day and realize you've been playing video games for hours and haven't even touched your homework? Preparation and staying on top of details will help you live each day mission possible.

It's About the End Goal

The grind may not be exciting. Often it stinks. The hours are long and painful. I've learned that not many people come along for that part of the journey. It's more fun to show up for the games, the concerts, the rescues, and the galas. Few show up when the blood, sweat, and tears are being ground out. But that's a story for another time.

One person who has lived each day with joy and grace in order to fulfill his mission is my dad. As I said in chapter 2, his mission is to preach the gospel to every person in the Philippines. I'll never forget how when I was growing up I'd wake up and go downstairs for breakfast, and my dad would always be sitting at the table reading his Bible and other study material. I believe his consistency and the passion he's had for his calling and his life over the years have had the most positive influence on me. Decades later, he is still consistent and passionate. He maintains stellar focus and unmatched energy. Despite his age and being diagnosed with Parkinson's disease, he continues to drive forward with passion and intensity. He doesn't let fatigue stop him. Even as his body is depleted of energy, he presses forward and travels back and forth from the United States to the Philippines to fulfill what God has called him to do. I pray I have the same type of stamina Dad has when I reach his age.

You know why Dad is this way? It's not because he is Superman or was born with a massive amount of energy or an inner drive that most of us weren't naturally blessed with. It's because he invests himself into the mission and works hard at it because he knows the payoff is worth it.

During the time I was writing this book, I held a staff retreat for my team at the foundation. I thought it would be cool to have Dad come out for the afternoon and answer some questions our staff had been asking. I study really hard to be prepared to lead our team, but I wanted Dad to be there because he has so much to offer in that regard.

Not only was Dad there to answer some really hard questions

(which he did for hours), but he also helped the team practice how to share the gospel with others. The gospel is important to us at TTF. In fact, it's the most important message we as Christians will share in our whole lives. Peter tells us, "Always [be] ready to make a defense to everyone who asks you to give an account for the hope that is in you, but with gentleness and respect" (1 Peter 3:15). After offering some coaching pointers on how to "give an account," Dad ran the team through some practice gospel presentations. Dad taught with respect, kindness, and patience—even when one of the presenters forgot to mention the Resurrection entirely (which is a pretty important piece of a gospel presentation, if you ask me). Dad did an amazing job and shared so much love and wisdom with our team. I could not have been prouder.

When I walked Dad to his car that afternoon, I thanked him from the bottom of my heart. I'll never forget what he told me as we talked about the meeting. "I stayed up until 4 a.m. studying the book of James." This is coming from a man who has read the book of James—and the entire Bible, for that matter—probably a thousand times. He was so invested in this staff retreat session and the lives of those who would be in attendance that he put in hours and hours of studying something he had already studied. And he was more than happy and willing to put in the work.

Let's talk about hard work for a minute. A work ethic is pointless without a purpose. Working hard is not the end goal; we work hard to get to the end goal. I know that not everyone is doing exactly what he or she dreams of doing every minute of every day, but we should still pursue our responsibilities with excellence. The Bible tells us, "Do your work heartily, as for the Lord and not for people, knowing that it is from the Lord that you will receive the reward of the inheritance. It is the Lord Christ whom you serve" (Colossians 3:23–24). Even if where you are isn't where you want to be, God can still use you.

Sure, a great work ethic is something to be proud of, but if there's no purpose to it beyond self-achievement, it's essentially meaningless. Why would you work out twice a day or study most weekends or do any number of hard things without a good reason? It might seem crazy, but to me that's a waste of time. If you're a Christian, your purpose is ultimately to glorify God, right? To love and serve God and others. A great work ethic is valuable, but it has more meaning when it is connected to a higher purpose.

My dad is committed to his mission, and he was committed to making the most out of his time with my team. Instead of relying solely on his knowledge and experience, of which he had plenty, he prayed and studied for hours to be prepared to point each person present at that staff retreat to Jesus.

When I think of commitment, I see the face of Brandi, the foundation's vice president of ministries. She's worked with me for more than ten years. Not only do I highly value her as an esteemed member of our team, but I treasure her as a friend and confidante. If TTF had a heart, it would be Brandi. It's because she never turns off. She has embraced the grind with utmost commitment, compassion, and foresight. She's always ten steps ahead, so I never have to worry about a W15H coming unglued due to a complication within our control.

One of the many characteristics that make Brandi shine above others is her commitment to both our team and the families we serve. She has taught us through her example of what it means to be a prayer warrior. Camryn, who also works with us, says, "I've sat back and watched her seek the Lord on behalf of people countless times, whether that's those we are considering hiring or our W15H families. I can't tell you how often we were on a W15H together and she'd just stop and say, 'Let's pause and pray.' Brandi has taught me so much about the power of prayer. She is more than a boss; she is a mentor and a friend."

Kelsey, whom I previously mentioned in this chapter, often brags about Brandi's deep sense of loyalty. "She knows how to love well, and she has counted the cost of what that will take. She will not hesitate to rearrange her entire schedule to hop on a plane to the other side of the country to help someone who is sick or in need. Brandi has shown me what it means to go above and beyond in serving others."

Serve, give, love, and be kind to others—not just because it makes you a good person or it'll make you look good, but because it will shine the light of Jesus to a world of darkness.

Find the Right Balance

When you are committed to a mission, nothing can stop you. You know whose you are. You understand that your time on earth is limited, so you live with a sense of urgency. You focus on what you need to do now and what you need to do next. When you live with this level of commitment, some might describe you as *intense*.

If you watch, as an outsider, two NFL teams during a practice, you'll probably think both teams are working super hard. And you're probably right. But as an insider, you can see their work ethic on a much deeper level. You'll be able to tell the difference between the players who are practicing with an "I'm working hard and I'll probably be sore tomorrow" attitude versus an "I'm working hard and I'll probably not be able to move in the morning" attitude. The latter is the kind of intensity that makes a difference on and off the field.

Picture watching a presentation in class. The presenter is locked into the topic at hand. He or she doesn't care if the room is too hot or too cold, if the rest of the class is paying attention or not, or if it's almost lunchtime. Coaches Urban Meyer and Bill Belichick were the best at locking in with this kind of focus and intensity. It's not enough to make a presentation; you have to lock in and do your best at it. It's not enough to wake up and show up for class; you have to participate and be engaged and actually learn something. It's not enough to just get out of bed in the morning; you have to live with open eyes to see the needs, an open heart to love, and open hands to serve.

I want to inspire people to have that kind of intensity.

I was born a very intense guy. I'm rather competitive by nature. I rarely take downtime. I'm not saying it's not important, but I just don't do it much. Rest is good. God rested on the seventh day of creation. Rest is biblical. But one of my worst shortcomings is not stopping and resting and pausing. I'm getting better at it, though. (At least I think I am—maybe I'll have to ask Demi.)

Taking time off is definitely a challenge because I feel the weight of hurting people around the world. In my mind, if I take a vacation or watch a movie or read a book or do any number of things to unplug, that's one less boy or girl who gets faith, hope, and love. That's one less person who gets to receive a hug, gets lavished with love, or gets cared for. That kind of pressure weighs heavily on me, and even though I realize it's a weight that's not mine to carry, I struggle to let it go.

I'm working on finding the right balance between pursuing my mission with locked-in intensity and resting so I can recover enough to continue fighting with passion.

Balance is a funny word. I don't know if we get it right all the time. I haven't found a formula for that yet. (If you've got one, let me know.) What I think is most important is to step back, look at the big picture, and pray. What do you want your life to look like? What kind of person do you want to be? We're not meant to live perfect lives, but we were created to live mission-possible ones. And I believe the path of purpose has far fewer regrets.

9

Purpose in the Waiting

*God does not give us everything we want, but he does
fulfill all his promises . . . leading us along the best
and straightest paths to himself.*

—DIETRICH BONHOEFFER

A rock star once sang, "The waiting is the hardest part."[1] Just ask anyone waiting to fall in love, for answers to prayer, or for the test results, and I'm sure he or she will agree. The Bible is full of stories of heroes on brutal journeys of waiting. While the shepherd boy David is waiting to be crowned king of Israel, he is on the run from a king who wants him dead. The apostle Paul is in prison while waiting to preach the gospel in another part of the world. Noah is waiting for rain to come while fielding doubt and dirty looks.

The psalmist wrote, "Wait for the LORD; be strong and let your heart take courage; yes, wait for the LORD" (Psalm 27:14). I've already talked about the times when God may not fully uncover every detail of our mission plans, but what happens when life takes an unexpected turn? What happens when our plans or our expectations get turned upside down?

I'd like to introduce you to an incredible boy named Ethan Hallmark and his parents, Rachel and Matt. This chapter is different from the rest. It contains a story I feel deserves more than just a few paragraphs. Before I give you a peek into this unbelievable illustration of one of the most courageous boys I have ever met, the most important thing I can tell you is this: Don't waste your waiting.

Let me say that again: Don't waste your waiting.

As you wait for God to show you where to go or what to do or an answer to prayer, He can and will use you right here and right now: at home, at school, at practice, at games, when you're working, when you're at rest. Purpose is always present, even in the waiting.

Nine-year-old Ethan had often complained about stomach pain, but it never seemed that big a deal until he was doubled over in pain on vacation. His parents took him to a doctor. "It's nothing serious," they were told, and they returned home with a prescription for a constipation medicine. But Ethan's pain got worse, and the medicine didn't help at all.

Two or three days later, Ethan was playing baseball in an All-Star game in Arlington, Texas. His mother remembers not being able to take her eyes off him as he crouched low in center field, legs spread wide. His hands gripped his thighs as he gritted his teeth in what looked like pain. But when the ball came flying toward him, Ethan instinctively sprang up in the air, his arm shooting high. The ball smacked hard into his thick leather glove as he smashed into the fence right behind him. The crowd went wild. Ethan sank to the ground, then slowly got up. It was the best final-out catch, but the boy couldn't enjoy the moment. He saw stars, and from what he later told his mother, it felt like an arsenal of knives were piercing into his legs and gut. Instead of celebrating with his cheering coaches and teammates in the dugout, Ethan hobbled off the field toward his mother. "Take me home," he begged his mom.

Within forty-eight hours, a doctor's visit, a CT scan, and a biopsy uncovered the source of Ethan's pain. On June 30, 2010, Ethan was diagnosed with stage IV, high-risk-of-relapse unfavorable-histology neuroblastoma, an aggressive form of pediatric cancer.

Rachel remembers the moment just before Ethan learned the diagnosis. "It's cancer, isn't it," he said. But what he said next was unexpected. "Well, I have hope. What do I have to do to get rid of it?"

Ethan spent the next year and a half at the oncology clinic or in the hospital. He endured intense treatment, including chemo, radiation, and surgeries. I was amazed to hear what Ethan had to say about one treatment. Honestly, if I had been in the same situation, I don't know if I could have responded like he did. He said,

Immunotherapy was the worst part of my treatment. The pain was so horrible, especially when it felt like I was on fire. I'd tell myself that Jesus suffered so much more than I ever have and He suffered for me. I knew I could finish the treatment.

Seven months into that first year of treatment, having lost weight, his hair, and almost all of his hearing in his right ear, he told Rachel, "Mom, you know what my favorite part of the Bible is? It's where it talks about the light conquering the darkness. You know, even the smallest amount of light can beat the darkest darkness." What a spiritual warrior.

When scans were done on September 24, 2011, fifteen months after Ethan's initial diagnosis, there was good news—a miracle! Ethan was 100 percent cancer-free! That day, Ethan's mom wrote this on her blog:

> Matt and I are forever thankful to our Maker not only for defeating Ethan's cancer but, more importantly, for defeating death for us. We don't know the future for Ethan, nor does anyone their own. However, we know that he is a living miracle!

Two weeks after Ethan learned he was in remission, he gave a talk in his school about perseverance and even showed the students the ten-inch scar on his abdomen where doctors removed the tumor. In his speech, he defined *perseverance* as "having a purpose in life in spite of your difficulties, having a goal and never stopping until you achieve that goal." After Ethan explained what cancer is and the type of treatment he received, he began to encourage his classmates:

> In spite of the difficulty of cancer, I had a purpose. My purpose was to never give up. My faith told me that in any

circumstance, the light would always beat the darkness. No matter how dark cancer was, the light would always shine through the darkness. Some of you might be facing problems right now, like bullying or not making the sports team. How can you overcome those difficulties? By persevering, by having a purpose. You have to know that you are special and loved, that God loves you.

Ethan celebrated his eleventh birthday on January 23, 2012, in remission. But two months later, the cancer came back, this time in the hard bone of his right arm, spanning nearly the length of his forearm, and also in the bone in his upper left arm and near his bladder. Here is what Ethan, at eleven years old, wrote a few days after the confirmed relapse:

Some people have been telling me it's okay to yell at God over my cancer relapse. They say God can take my anger. I've been thinking about that: Why would I yell at God when He sent His only Son to die for me? Am I upset? Of course! Our God knows my heart, and He knows that I am hurting. Relapsed neuroblastoma is nothing to be happy about. God has healed me once, and I know He will heal me again either way. But why would I be angry at God when He carried me all this way? Instead of being angry at God, I'm praising Him for the many blessings I have. I'm asking Jesus to heal me from my cancer and to give me strength to endure this treatment. God is going to be with me through this whole difficult journey. He is always there.

The Hallmarks' motto during this time? REMISSION POSSIBLE.

A few months later, doctors removed five neuroblastoma tumors.

"How quickly will the tumors grow back?" Rachel asked the oncologist.

"Rapidly," the doctor replied.

While no one can predict the path that neuroblastoma will take, one thing was certain: Ethan was not afraid to die. This is what he told his mom during a tough conversation:

I'm not afraid to die because in the big picture, we are all going to die. I might be eleven and another person one hundred. It doesn't matter. We will all die someday. I don't want to die at an early age. Who does? But I am not afraid to die because I get to spend eternity with God. Some people are afraid to die because they don't know there is eternal life afterwards. Heaven is pure joy, where there is no pain, no suffering, and no evil. I will be in the presence of God and Jesus. As great as we think it is, it will be infinitely better. So why would I be afraid to die?

I met Ethan, his parents, and his grandfather on September 16, 2012, while I was playing an away game in Pittsburg for the New York Jets. He made a tremendous impact on me and everyone he met mainly because of his sweet spirit and love for Jesus. I'll never forget how before the game Ethan asked if he could pray for me. His faith was unshakable. After the game, we spent so much time chatting in the locker room that I was late in catching the bus back home. I couldn't help it! I didn't want my conversation with him to end. I truly enjoyed every minute I spent with Ethan and his family, and I can tell you that he encouraged me a lot more than I encouraged him.

Though they knew the war was far from over, the Hallmarks received a great report a little more than a week after I met with Ethan. All his scans came back clear. Ethan's second remission from cancer was confirmed. He said this about the news:

Thank you for all your continued prayers. God has answered them. Please continue to pray that the cancer never comes back and that I stay in remission. I am so thankful for the healing that God has done in my life. God is so good. God has brought me to the point that science said I wouldn't get to. I am dependent on Jesus, and I'm prepared for whatever life throws at me. Cancer may knock me down at times, but God is the ultimate builder. None of us know what the future holds, but in all things we know God has special plans for every one of us. We know that if we have faith, we have eternity with our heavenly Father. It is always a win-win situation for those who believe in God.

Ups and downs followed, and although the cancer eventually returned, Ethan continued to pray, fight, and believe. When he relapsed the second time, he wrote the following:

I am hopeful that God will perform another miracle. I feel like I had only a short break from this disease, just like when David was chased by Saul. As soon as Saul died, David's own sons started chasing after him. Even though I am being chased endlessly by this disease, God is right beside me through it all. Running this marathon is not easy, but I focus on the goal of eternal life. God loved David, but David still endured trials of many kinds. God was always there for David, and He is always there for me. Even though I have cancer, God will not abandon or forsake me. No matter what happens, this disease cannot separate me from the love of God.

Four years after Ethan was first diagnosed with neuroblastoma, though radiation was attacking the cancer, new growth was showing up. Ethan and his parents continued to have some tough conversations. Ethan said this to his mom in one of them:

I know cancer is starting to take over my body. I know my body is broken. I hoped God would give me more time on earth, but I'm not afraid of dying or losing my life. I'm just really sad for you and Dad. I don't want you both to hurt like this.

Six days before his body would finally be rid of the disease and he would meet Jesus face to face, Ethan said this to his parents:

My biggest fear isn't dying. My biggest fear is that others will blame God for my death and not believe in Him. I don't want people angry at God or even blaming Him. I mean, there is so much more than only this life. Just because He didn't heal me on earth doesn't mean He won't heal me in heaven.

On September 26, 2014, Ethan fell into the arms of Jesus. He was welcomed home and finally made whole.

When Ethan was four years old, Rachel told her husband, Matt, she had a feeling their oldest son would grow up to be a pastor. And, in a sense, he did. Once he was diagnosed, Ethan saw and accepted, with grace and hope, his mission of sharing the gospel through his suffering. Over a third of his life was spent in the trenches of cancer as he faced endless rounds of high-dose chemo, stem-cell transplants, multiple surgeries, more than one hundred days of radiation, and endless travel for trial after trial. On the surface, his life was marked by suffering, but that was only part of the fight. Ethan wanted people to know the truth that the glory to come, the glory found in the priceless gift of Jesus Christ, far surpassed any amount of suffering endured in this temporary world: "I wouldn't trade my relationship with Jesus for anything . . . nothing at all." Ethan wanted a life that represented the size of the prize at the end of this life on earth.

Three months before Ethan passed into heaven, he spent a week at a family camp in Colorado. Every morning a counselor set aside time to talk with him and two other teen boys. One day, this counselor and the three boys discussed what gifts they felt God had given them. Perhaps they were good at serving others or were compassionate. When it was Ethan's turn, he was quick to answer. "My gift is cancer."

Ethan never wanted to die. He didn't enjoy the suffering his gift brought him. He didn't experience joy when his body was pumped with radiation, or his nerves were on fire, or his mouth was full of so many sores he could barely eat, or when he had lost his hearing. But Ethan recognized he could use his gift to reach others for Christ. And every single day, whether he was in pain or not, Ethan did just that. He did it by how he chose to handle and view his suffering. He did it by encouraging his family, his friends, fellow cancer warriors, and strangers he may one day meet again. Ethan's parents received countless phone calls, emails, and letters from people, young and old, who shared how Ethan's life influenced their own. Some were so inspired by his story of unshakable faith in the face of death that they made the decision to trust in or rededicate their lives to Jesus.

While Ethan waited to beat cancer, he used the darkness—what the Enemy meant to destroy him—to bring others closer to the light of Christ.

Ethan, mission accomplished!

How was this young man, only nine years old at the time of diagnosis and barely a teenager by the time he crossed over into heaven, able to say that cancer was his gift? How could he keep such a grounded perspective of his identity in Jesus while his body suffered in unimaginable ways? How did he maintain gratitude during the last few years of his life while he rode a roller coaster of the cancer's remission and return? Ethan knew God was in control, so he could trust Him in the waiting.

I don't know what you are waiting for, but I promise you there is always purpose in the waiting. You may think your life will start when you get your driver's license, graduate high school, go to college, or get your dream job. Purpose doesn't show up when that thing finally comes to pass because there is purpose in everything. Because God is always in the present, it's always possible to matter, to have meaning, and to make it count—right now.

Don't wait for purpose to find you someday. Say yes to what God says is possible for and through you in the present.

10

Your Life Counts

I have one life and one chance to
make it count for something.

—JIMMY CARTER

My buddy Ethan said a number of profound things. One of them was, "It doesn't matter if you live to be one or one hundred. What matters is what you did for Christ."

One of my biggest goals in life is to get to heaven one day and hear God tell me, "Well done, good and faithful servant" (Matthew 25:23, ESV).

The world defines success in many different ways. Maybe it's accumulating a certain number of followers on social media, becoming famous for an accomplishment, or crossing off the checklist of your detailed five-year plan. I hope you reach your goals and get the gold star or hold the trophy up high. But there's something limiting about success as defined by the world. It's self-oriented. The world is going to tell me that success is about opportunity, fame, and fortune for Tim Tebow. It might say that success is about praise and promotion. In other words, success is about "me." It's about who I am and what I did and do. It's ours to hold on to. And, ultimately, that kind of success is not fulfilling. It will always be missing something or Someone.

God gives us the opportunity to turn success into significance. We can use what we've been given for others. Success in itself isn't a bad thing. There's never been a day in my life in which I've wanted to lose, whether that's a game or a deal. But I also know that if I allow success to be used in only a self-fulfilling way, I won't have ultimate purpose.

Significance, however, is about others—loving and serving people. One of the greatest questions you can ask yourself is, *Does my life change other people's lives for the better?*

When you're focused on others, when you bring the love and light of Jesus to hurting people, your life counts for more than a title people will forget or an achievement someone will probably surpass in time. Years ago, I heard someone say that one of the greatest tragedies in life is to look back one day and say, "I was successful in things that don't matter." I am writing this chapter so that you live today with tomorrow in mind. I don't want your end goal to be about praise, promotion, and applause; I want it to be about people, purpose, and passion.

I preach all the time about living with significance. I try to live it out. That said, I battle daily with doing so. Living with significance is one of the hardest things to do because it doesn't take much to veer off track. I'm running the race for God, and then all of a sudden one self-serving thought creeps into my head and then I'm running the race for me. I'm constantly trying to keep my head and my heart in the right place, where significance is always my priority. It's not easy, but it's worth it.

Every single one of us has a chance to make a difference. We have the opportunity, the ability, and the capacity to do something to build the kingdom of God. It's not because we're great or qualified or successful; it's mission possible because we've teamed up with the God of this universe. When we take aim into the future and live lives of significance, anything is possible.

Make the Choice

Before we start dreaming about what's possible, however, we must remind ourselves of something. Even as we lock into significance over success, the results are beyond our control. We are not responsible for the outcome of our prayers. We allow God to open or close the doors He chooses for us. We allow His will to be done in our lives and the lives of others.

We do, however, have the power of choice. We can choose our attitude. We can choose in whom we put our hope. We can choose in what or whom we trust.

Remember Jeneil in chapter 5? She was a volunteer at Night to Shine whose daughter Rhema struggles with special needs. Rhema was diagnosed with autism, apraxia, and a seizure disorder. For years, Jeneil battled anger and depression. *Where is God in all this?* she wondered. *How will I manage? What does the future look like for Rhema?* In the midst of this uncertainty, Jeneil knew that something had to give.

In a letter she wrote to me, Jeneil said, "Even though I could not see what God was doing, I had to make a choice to believe that He was and is faithful. My daughter's struggles did not go away. Even now she can still have very hard days. But God was doing a healing work in our family, and in many ways, it had nothing to do with autism."

Before Rhema was born, Jeneil and her husband chose Romans 10:8–9 as their daughter's theme verse. Jeneil has recited it to her every night at bedtime for the past fourteen years: " 'The word is near you, in your mouth and in your heart' (that is, the word of faith that we proclaim); because, if you confess with your mouth that Jesus is Lord and believe in your heart that God raised him from the dead, you will be saved" (ESV).

Because Rhema had apraxia and was nonverbal, it was impossible for her to communicate. Jeneil longed to have a conversation with Rhema—for her daughter to share why she was upset, what she wanted to wear, what her favorite color was, what made her feel a certain way, and what Jeneil could do to make her feel better. There were signs that Rhema understood far more than doctors had led them to believe. For example, her dad used to put red Crystal Light packets in his water bottles. When he deployed to Kuwait, Jeneil stopped buying them. The next day, on her iPad, Rhema started tapping a picture symbol of tomato juice. She would do that almost daily. She'd never had tomato juice before, but Jeneil quickly bought her a big bottle of it. When Rhema tried it, she grimaced. It was not what she wanted. But day after day, she kept tapping the picture of tomato juice. It wasn't until one year later, when Rhema's dad came home from overseas with his

Crystal Light packets, that Jeneil figured it out. Rhema tapped a picture of tomato juice and eagerly grabbed a packet of the beverage mix and a water bottle. Amazing! Tomato juice was the closest image she could find to what she wanted. That was one sign that convinced Rhema's parents that she had far more understanding than they had thought.

In 2015, Rhema began a teaching method called rapid prompting method (RPM). A person trained in this technique uses an alphabet board or a tablet and, with words or gestures, prompts a person with autism to point to or tap letters, words, and pictures. Pointing was at first a challenge for Rhema because she lacked the motor skills to form her fingers into a point, but Jeneil was determined to work with her daughter using this method.

Mother and daughter first studied the book of Exodus. Jeneil would read from this book in the Bible, ask Rhema a question about it, and then encourage her to point to a choice, like *y-e-s* or *n-o*.

The two read the Bible together, one word at a time. With each letter spelled out, the Word of God began to write itself onto their hearts. It was a painfully slow process. Each word consumed them both.

Jeneil sensed that Rhema identified with Moses, a man who battled his insecurities because of a speech impediment. A man who didn't think he was capable of public speaking, let alone leading the nation of Israel out of slavery in Egypt. A man who was afraid to step into the mission God was calling him to fulfill.

Something in Rhema's spirit seemed to be moved when her

mother read how Moses argued with God about why he wasn't the man to lead Israel out of Egypt. "I have never been eloquent, neither in the past nor since you have spoken to your servant. I am slow of speech and tongue" (Exodus 4:10, NIV). Moses's protests didn't change God's opinion of the mission; God reminded the stuttering man of His abiding presence.

As Jeneil continued to read through the fourth chapter of Exodus, which detailed the excuses Moses presented before suggesting God find someone better qualified for the job, Jeneil asked Rhema, "What did God say to Moses's objections?" and wrote down different choices on a piece of paper.

Rhema paused. She lifted her trembling hand, clenched into a tight fist, as one finger extended beyond the others in a beautiful, hard-won point. She pressed down on the words *I will be with you.* They may not have been audible words, but Rhema understood the question. She may not have been able to speak with her mouth, but her comprehension was on point.

After a full year of studying with her mother every night, Rhema spelled her first sentence of open communication. They'd been studying a lesson on the Lord's Prayer. Jeneil asked her daughter, "What did you pray for?"

As her mother held up the stencil board, Rhema pointed to and spelled, "I h-a-v-e m-y v-o-i-c-e."

Jeneil's heart raced. *Could it be true? Had she imagined what had just happened?* "Can you do that again, Rhema? Can you tell me again what you prayed for?"

Once again, "I h-a-v-e m-y v-o-i-c-e."

Jeneil couldn't believe what she was seeing:

It was the most incredible moment of my life because I knew that God had done it. And the moment she spelled that she prayed to have her voice, she had her voice. God answered her prayer then and there. Our God is a God with perfect plans. He sees and hears and knows us. He comes down to deliver us. He teaches us what to say. He performs wonders in our midst. And He is with us.

Two years after beginning RPM, Rhema wrote these beautiful words:

How I love Jesus.

I am so happy He saved me. . . .

I think having autism might make some think I have a sad life. That is not true. I am happy that I am fearfully and wonderfully made. I am thankful for my autism because it teaches me to trust God. My body is not something I can trust, but the God who made me is. He not only made me autistic; He made me not able to speak with my mouth but with my heart.

Can you love God when your body betrays you every day? *You can.*

So much of my trouble with my motor skills comes from sensory overload. It makes me want to jump out of my skin. It is mostly awful to feel this way, but I know the Lord made my body.

So I even will trust Him in this good and mostly mean body. . . .

My hope is in the Lord. I thank Him. For He is always good.[1]

Jeneil made the best choices she could make in one of the hardest times in her life: She chose to fix her eyes on Jesus. She chose to be all in, mothering her children and helping Rhema find her voice. And Rhema? Well, even though the world may see her as the least and the last, she trusted that the Creator had fearfully and wonderfully made her body.

We, too, have the power to choose. We can choose to believe that God has a plan and a purpose for our lives. We can choose to look at our disadvantages as opportunities. We can choose, like Ethan, to fight our battles on this earth with faith in Jesus Christ.

Will you make the choice to begin to see what's mission possible when you trust in Jesus? When you make the choice to say yes, you will change a life. One or many. It doesn't matter—that's up to God.

The choices we make today will have an impact tomorrow. Whether it's how we spend our time or treat other people, choices that seem small can have great significance. Our choices can give others the courage they need to do something they had never planned on or even imagined they would do.

Be the Reason

In 2020, we at TTF helped sponsor our first Night to Shine in Paris, hosted by the Jérôme Lejeune Foundation. The French capital, nicknamed the City of Lights, is nothing short of beautiful.

Demi and I marveled at the city's magnificent views, its labyrinth of cobblestone streets, and of course the Eiffel Tower, which bursts with golden sparkles of lights for a few minutes at the beginning of every hour from sundown to 1 A.M. But all that magical wonder would pale in comparison to the beauty I would witness from a young woman later that evening.

As Night to Shine guests began their celebratory jaunt down a red carpet swarmed with cheering people lining the edges, I noticed a woman in a wheelchair being rolled down. Dressed in all black, she wore a red baseball cap that covered the crown of her beautiful tight curls. As she sat in the wheelchair, a smile swelled from cheek to cheek. Her rigid hands met each other in a spastic, awkward rhythm, over and over, the entire length of the red carpet as she squealed in utter delight at the crowd that celebrated her with shouts and applause.

Fifteen minutes later, this young woman was back—this time without a wheelchair. No, she wasn't healed. Her ability to walk didn't change, but she seemed to be so motivated by the cheering volunteers that she had to at least try. With the help of a volunteer, she made her second entrance walking down the red carpet. The beautiful scene brought tears to my eyes. I wasn't sure what disability she had, but she obviously had a hard time walking. She'd swing one stiff leg up in the air (parallel to the floor), stomp it down on the ground, and do the same thing with the other leg, kind of like a soldier's march. As she marched forward with confidence, her warm smile illuminated more radiance than the Eiffel Tower.

When I think about that young woman, I can still picture her glowing face, her head bobbing up and down with glee as her smile curled up into her eyes. She seemed astonished as she soaked in the attention lavished on her. I've seen this look on many Night to Shine guests over the years. They can't process how loved and celebrated they are even for one night. It's overwhelming for some. And I like to think that for a few short minutes, this woman felt so cherished and encouraged that she decided to try to walk. She may have needed help. It may not have looked like the type of walking many of us are used to seeing. But as this woman raised one stiff leg up and then another, she seemed to gain more confidence with every step. And if it was even possible, her smile swelled further, drowning her face in the purest kind of joy. I had just spent an incredible day in a breathtaking city with my gorgeous wife, but what shone the brightest that day was that woman walking down the red carpet.

Watching her made me think of something: I want to be the reason that people think they *can*. I want to be the reason that people have a brighter day. I want to be the reason that people get closer to Jesus. I hope you do too.

What's inside you that gives you the reason others will believe they can? Success? Maybe. Definitely significance. But even more than that, if you are a believer, it's Jesus. And because of Jesus, namely His death and resurrection, we have the hope and glory of living not for the temporary but for what's eternal.

Infinite Perspective

To live for the eternal is to live and do things a little differently. Living mission possible means living with an eternal mindset, knowing that our work on earth is accomplishing something of eternal value.

Paul knew this. He wrote, "I have fought the good fight, I have finished the course, I have kept the faith; in the future there is reserved for me the crown of righteousness, which the Lord, the righteous Judge, will award to me on that day; and not only to me, but also to all who have loved His appearing" (2 Timothy 4:7–8).

If we live for the here and now, of course we're going to focus on success and fun and living our best lives now. Why wouldn't we want to do whatever we want when we want and how we want to do it? But, as the Bible tells us, this isn't our home.

> Our citizenship is in heaven, from which we also eagerly wait for a Savior, the Lord Jesus Christ; who will transform the body of our lowly condition into conformity with His glorious body, by the exertion of the power that He has even to subject all things to Himself. (Philippians 3:20–21)

We can't get too comfortable with life on earth. We won't be here forever. What matters more than the fun we have or the stuff we accumulate is what we did with the time we were given. The Bible tells us, "If you have been raised with Christ, keep seeking the things that are above, where Christ is, seated at the right hand of God. Set your minds on the things that are above, not on the things that are on earth" (Colossians 3:1–2).

Instead of seeking success in our own lives, we seek to bring faith, hope, and love to those needing a brighter day in their dark-

est hour of need. That's not just our foundation's mission statement; that's our hearts' cry. I don't know what your mission is,
but I hope it's one that makes your heart long for Jesus and love
people.

As children of God, we not only get to live forever with Jesus
but also get to share that hope and that light with others now so
they, too, can live each day focused on the eternal.

Did you know you were made for eternity? Did you know that
this is not your home? My hope and prayer for you is that you are
able to say that heaven is your forever home. Jesus came to this
earth to bring you good news of great joy. He died for you with
eternity in mind. With Him, we can have an abundant life on
earth. In riches and power? Maybe. In meaning and significance?
Absolutely!

We may not be blessed with Tom Cruise's stunt skills. I can't
sing, and maybe you can't play football. But there's one thing we
can all do: Because of the work Jesus did for us on the cross and
through the Resurrection, we can each make our lives count.

We live mission possible because the tough part of the mission
has already been accomplished by Jesus. Yes, we have to make
hard choices every day. We have to sacrifice. We have to grind out
the work. And sometimes the days and the moments are just
plain hard. We're going to mess up and stumble and be disap-
pointed along the way. I know this might sound discouraging, but
really, it's not.

Remember the words of Jesus: "In the world you have tribulation, but take courage; I have overcome the world" (John 16:33).
I love the Christian Standard Bible translation: "Be courageous! I

have conquered the world." When you make the decision to trust in Jesus, you also are a conqueror! (see Romans 8:37).

Life can be so painful at times that it may seem impossible to stay mission possible. But when we maintain an eternal perspective and remind ourselves that Jesus took us from

old to new,
    dead to alive,
        sin to righteousness,
            slave to son or daughter,
                bondage to freedom,
                    darkness to light,
                        lost to found,

we begin to live lives of significance.

In the movie *Gladiator*, the Roman general Maximus exhorts his troops with this: "What we do in life echoes in eternity."[2]

Make your life count. This doesn't have much to do with your skill or success or talents. Rather, it has everything to do with the unique calling and purpose God has given you that He has already equipped you for. It has to do with what He has made mission possible.

Now, let's go live that out!

A Special Invitation

I f you have just finished this book and you don't know Jesus in the personal way I've been describing but would like to, keep reading.

Jesus loves you so much that He paid for all the wrong you've ever done. He died on a cross for you and for me, and three days later, He conquered death and rose from the dead. If you believe that, wherever you are, tell Him right now:

Dear Jesus, I believe that You died on the cross and that You rose from the dead. I know that I am a sinner. Please come into my heart and forgive me of my sin. Thank You for forgiving me and trading the old for the new, the darkness for the light. Jesus, I love You and I want to live for You. I give You my life. Thank You for saving me. Thank You for giving me a home in heaven where I will come and live with You forever one day. Thank You for taking my place and paying my debt. In Jesus's name. Amen.

When you make the decision to trust in Jesus, you are adopted into the family of God. And because God is now your Father in heaven, that makes you my brother or sister.

Welcome to the fam!

If you have already made the decision to trust in Jesus and would like to commit to making your life count, why don't you tell Him right now? Say this prayer with me:

Dear Jesus, I believe I can live a mission-possible life because Your mission was accomplished. Give me the courage to do whatever You have called me to do. Remind me that because You have overcome the world, I can do all things that are put before me. Thank You that I get to live mission possible. Amen.

Notes

Introduction

1. J. R. R. Tolkien, *The Hobbit* (New York: Ballantine Books, 1965), 4.

2. Tim Tebow Foundation, www.timtebowfoundation.org /ministries.

3. Reed Tucker, "How Tom Cruise Clung to a Plane in the New 'Mission: Impossible,'" *New York Post*, July 25, 2015, https://nypost.com/2015/07/25/how-tom-cruise-clung-to -a-plane-in-the-new-mission-impossible.

1: Mission Proposal, Mission Purpose

The chapter epigraph is taken from Rick Perry, "Remarks Announcing Campaign Suspension," American Rhetoric (speech, Columbia International University, North Charleston, S.C., January 19, 2012), www.americanrhetoric.com /speeches/rickperrycampaignsuspension.htm.

1. Will Burns, "Research Proves That the Storyteller Is Valued More Than Anyone Else in a Society," *Forbes*, December 7, 2017, www.forbes.com/sites/willburns/2017/12/07

/research-proves-that-the-storyteller-is-valued-more-than
-anyone-in-a-society/?sh=156c82cc7a15.

2. Lin-Manuel Miranda, quoted in Edward Delman, "How
Lin-Manuel Miranda Shapes History," *Atlantic,* September
29, 2015, www.theatlantic.com/entertainment/archive/2015
/09/lin-manuel-miranda-hamilton/408019.

3. Lin-Manuel Miranda, "Non-stop," *Hamilton: An American
Musical,* Atlantic, 2015.

2: God Possible, Purpose Possible

1. John H. Walton and Craig S. Keener, *NIV Cultural Back-
grounds Study Bible: Bringing to Life the Ancient World of Scripture*
(Grand Rapids, Mich.: Zondervan, 2016), 2078.

3: Right Where You Are

The chapter epigraph is taken from Theodore Roosevelt,
Theodore Roosevelt: An Autobiography (New York: Scribner,
1922), 337.

1. "Giving Thanks Can Make You Happier," Harvard Health
Publishing, August 14, 2021, www.health.harvard.edu
/healthbeat/giving-thanks-can-make-you-happier.

4: Mission-Possible Superpowers

The chapter epigraph is taken from R. C. Sproul, *In the Presence of God: Devotional Readings on the Attributes of God*
(Nashville: Thomas Nelson, 1999), 24.

Notes

1. Kevin Hall, *Aspire: Discovering Your Purpose Through the Power of Words* (New York: HarperCollins ebooks, 2009), 68, Kindle.

5: Purpose in the Present

The chapter epigraph is taken from Vincent van Gogh, "To Theo van Gogh, The Hague, Sunday, 22 October 1882," Van Gogh Museum, 1990, http://vangoghletters.org/vg /letters/let274/letter.html.

1. Michael Raupp, "What Do Butterflies Do When It Rains?," *Scientific American*, June 19, 2006, www .scientificamerican.com/article/what-do-butterflies-do-wh.
2. Krishna Ramanujan, "Armor on Butterfly Wings Protects Against Heavy Rain," *Cornell Chronicle*, June 8, 2020, https:// news.cornell.edu/stories/2020/06/armor-butterfly-wings -protects-against-heavy-rain.

6: Purpose in the Resistance

The chapter epigraph is taken from Sophocles, *Electra*, 418 B.C.

1. Jordi Quoidbach and Elizabeth W. Dunn, "Give It Up: A Strategy for Combating Hedonic Adaptation," *Social Psychological and Personality Science* 4, no. 5 (January 2013): 563–68, www.researchgate.net/publication/258189739_Give_It_Up _A_Strategy_for_Combating_Hedonic_Adaptation.
2. Alexis de Tocqueville, *Democracy in America*, Library of America (New York: Literary Classics of the United States, 2004), 617.

3. Dave Ramsey, *The Total Money Makeover: A Proven Plan for Financial Fitness,* Classic Edition (Nashville: Thomas Nelson, 2013), 106.

4. Robert Sanders, "Researchers Find Out Why Some Stress Is Good for You," *Berkeley News,* UC Berkeley, April 16, 2013, https://news.berkeley.edu/2013/04/16/researchers-find-out-why-some-stress-is-good-for-you.

7: Elevate Convictions over Emotions

The chapter epigraph is taken from C. S. Lewis, *Mere Christianity* (New York: Macmillan, 1960), 117.

1. Helen Keller, *The Story of My Life: With Her Letters (1887–1901) and a Supplementary Account of Her Education, Including Passages from the Reports and Letters of Her Teacher, Anne Mansfield Sullivan* (Garden City, N.Y.: Doubleday, 1921), 203.

2. David Jeremiah, "Believe: Get Your Mind Right," Sermons.Love, https://sermons.love/david-jeremiah/6972-david-jeremiah-believe-get-your-mind-right.html.

3. In order of appearance, see Isaiah 6:1–5; Psalm 11:7; 71:19; Deuteronomy 32:4; Daniel 9:9; Luke 6:36; Ephesians 2:4; 1 John 4:7–16; Psalm 69:16; 2 Timothy 2:13; Exodus 34:6; 2 Kings 13:23; Isaiah 49:13; 1 Chronicles 16:34; Mark 10:18; Proverbs 3:19; Romans 16:27.

8: Embrace the Grind

The chapter epigraph is taken from Martin Gilbert, *Winston S. Churchill,* vol. 3, *The Challenge of War, 1914–1916* (Hillsdale, Mich.: Hillsdale College Press, 2008).

Notes

1. Quoted in Chris Meikel, *26.2: A Marathon of Christian Devotions: Learning Life's Lessons Through Running* (Bloomington, Ind.: WestBow, 2014), xi.

9: Purpose in the Waiting

The chapter epigraph is taken from Dietrich Bonhoeffer, *Letters and Papers from Prison*, ed. Eberhard Bethge (London: SCM, 2001).

1. Tom Petty and the Heartbreakers, "The Waiting," *Hard Promises*, Backstreet, 1981.

10: Your Life Counts

The chapter epigraph is taken from Jim Wooten, "The Conciliator," *New York Times Magazine*, January 29, 1995, www.nytimes.com/1995/01/29/magazine/the-conciliator.html.

1. Rhema Russell, "How I Love Jesus," *Planting Roots* (blog), August 22, 2018, https://plantingroots.net/worship-wednesday-178.

2. *Gladiator*, directed by Ridley Scott (Universal City, Calif.: Universal Pictures, 2000).

PHOTO: © ADAM SZARMACK, MISSION DRIVEN STUDIOS

TIM TEBOW is a two-time national champion, Heisman Trophy winner, first-round NFL draft pick, and former professional baseball player. Tebow currently serves as a speaker, is a college football analyst with ESPN and the SEC Network, and is the author of five *New York Times* bestsellers, including *Shaken, Mission Possible, This Is the Day,* and the children's book *Bronco and Friends: A Party to Remember.* He is the founder and leader of the Tim Tebow Foundation (TTF), whose mission is to bring faith, hope, and love to those needing a brighter day in their darkest hour of need. Tim is married to Demi-Leigh Tebow (née Nel-Peters), a speaker, influencer, entrepreneur, and Miss Universe 2017. Tim and Demi live in Jacksonville, Florida, with their three dogs, Chunk, Kobe, and Paris.

www.timtebow.com
Facebook, Instagram, Twitter: @timtebow
LinkedIn: www.linkedin.com/in/timtebow15
TikTok: @timtebow_15

About the Type

This book was set in Albertina, a typeface created by Dutch calligrapher and designer Chris Brand (1921–98). Brand's original drawings, based on calligraphic principles, were modified considerably to conform to the technological limitations of typesetting in the early 1960s. The development of digital technology later allowed Frank E. Blokland (b. 1959) of the Dutch Type Library to restore the typeface to its creator's original intentions.

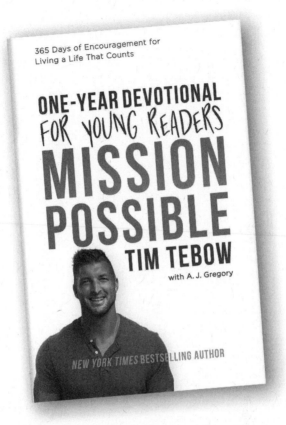

365 Days of Encouragement for Living a Life That Counts

ONE-YEAR DEVOTIONAL FOR YOUNG READERS

MISSION POSSIBLE

TIM TEBOW

with A. J. Gregory

NEW YORK TIMES BESTSELLING AUTHOR

This 365-day devotional from the *New York Times* bestselling author and athlete inspires young Christians to find their mission and pursue a bold, bright, fulfilling life—every single day.

TimTebow.com/MissionPossible

WATERBROOK

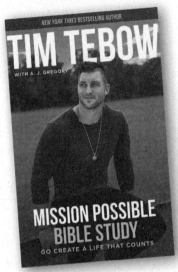
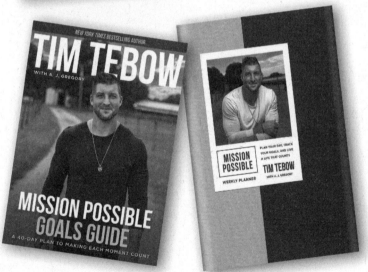

Also from Tim Tebow!

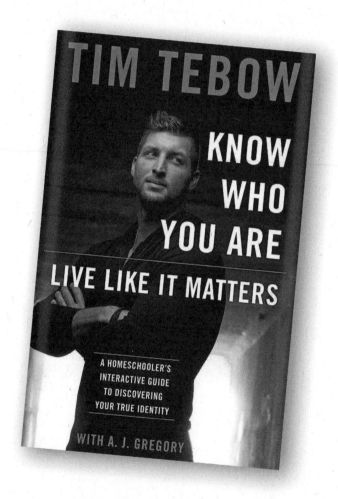

WMBooks.com/KnowWhoYouAre